Bones. —
bought @
Science Museum Boston

Aug. 1990

THE SEVEN WONDERS
of the
ANCIENT WORLD

The SEVEN WONDERS of the ANCIENT WORLD

Peter A. Clayton
and
Martin J. Price

DORSET PRESS
New York

First published in 1988
by Routledge
11 New Fetter Lane, London EC4P 4EE, England
Set in 10/12pt Bembo
by Columns Ltd, Reading
Editorial material and chapters 1, 3 and 7
© Peter A. Clayton and Martin J. Price 1988
All other material © Routledge 1988

This edition published by Dorset Press,
a division of Marboro Books Corporation,
by arrangement with Routledge
1989 Dorset Press

ISBN 0-88029-393-4

Printed in the United States of America

M 9 8 7 6 5 4 3 2

CONTENTS

ILLUSTRATIONS

ABOUT THE AUTHORS
AND CONTRIBUTORS

Peter A. Clayton, FLA, FSA, FRNS, is Editorial Consultant to B.A. Seaby Ltd, Numismatists to HM The Queen, and was formerly Managing Editor of British Museum Publications Ltd. He is an Honorary Member of the Institute of Archaeology of London University, Past President of the British Association of Numismatic Societies and Chairman of several archaeological societies. He lectures widely in England and Europe on Egyptian art and antiquities and visits Egypt every year by invitation as a guest lecturer. Author of *The Rediscovery of Ancient Egypt* (also published in French, German, Italian and Spanish); *Archaeological Sites of Britain* (2nd edn); *Treasures of Ancient Rome*; editor and principal contributor to *A Companion to Roman Britain*, and he revised, enlarged and picture edited *The Gods and Symbols of Ancient Egypt*. Has contributed many articles on ancient Egypt, numismatics and antiquity to various encyclopedias and learned journals.

Martin J. Price, MA, PhD, FSA, is Deputy Keeper of the Department of Coins and Medals in the British Museum with curatorial responsibility for the coinage of the Greek world. Formerly Secretary of the Royal Numismatic Society, he founded their publication *Coin Hoards*, a series which co-ordinates internationally the recording of new coin finds. He has written and lectured widely in the field of ancient coinage. His major publications include several fascicules of the *Sylloge Nummorum Graecorum* and *Coins of the Macedonians*; he was co-author of *Archaic Greek Silver Coins: The Asyut Hoard*, and joint author, with Bluma Trell, of *Coins and Their Cities: Architecture on the Ancient Coins of Greece, Rome and Palestine*; he was the editor and a major contributor to *Coins: An Illustrated Survey from 650 B.C. to the Present Day*, and he contributes regularly to the learned journals on ancient numismatics.

Irving L. Finkel, BA, PhD, is an Assistant Keeper in the Department of Western Asiatic Antiquities in the British Museum with special responsibility for cuneiform texts. He is the author of many contributions to the learned journals on cuneiform and has a special interest in magical, medical and astronomical texts. Currently working on research on Professor T.G. Pinches and his collection and also engaged in fieldwork in Iraq.

Bluma L. Trell is Professor Emerita of Classics and Comparative Literature in New York University. She has written and lectured widely on the buildings that are represented on ancient coins. Her reconstruction of the Temple of Artemis at Ephesos is on permanent display with the material from the site in the British Museum. She is also well known for her work on the influence of the Phoenicians in the Western Mediterranean. She is the author of *The Temple of Artemis at Ephesos* and joint author, with Martin Price, of *Coins and Their Cities*.

Geoffrey B. Waywell, MA, PhD, FSA, is Professor of Classical Archaeology at King's College, University of London. His doctoral thesis concerned the emergence of landscape in Greek art and he has been closely concerned with the Danish excavations on the site of the Mausoleum at Bodrum (ancient Halicarnassus). He is the author of *The Free-Standing Sculptures of the Mausoleum at Halicarnassus in the British Museum*, the definitive catalogue.

Reynold Higgins, MA, LittD, FBA, FSA, was formerly Acting Keeper of the Department of Greek and Roman Antiquities in the British Museum and Chairman of the British School of Archaeology in Athens. The author of many books on Greek art and archaeology, notably the *Catalogue of Greek Terracottas in the British Museum* (2 vols); *Greek and Roman Jewellery*; *Minoan and Mycenaean Art*, etc., and numerous papers in the learned journals.

ACKNOWLEDGMENTS

The authors and publishers are grateful to the following sources for the illustrations listed. 1 Cartodraftel; 8, 71 Swan Hellenic Ltd; 9, 10, 11, 12, 14, 15, 16, 17, 25, 32, 36, 37, 39, 40, 47, 50, 56, 68, 69, 72, 75, 76, 77, 80, 82 Peter Clayton; 13, 41, 42, 63, 64, 70 Jock Shaw; 20, 21, 22, 23, 24, 53, 54, 55, 57, 58, 59, 60 The Trustees of the British Museum; 28 Professor D.J. Wiseman; 31 Bibliothèque Nationale, Paris; 33, 34, 35, 38 German Archaeological Institute, Athens; 43, 44, 81, 83 Mansell Collection, London; 48 Trinity College Library, Cambridge; 49 John D. Schiff (Staempfli Gallery, New York); 51 Geoffrey Waywell. Unacknowledged illustrations are from the authors' collections.

INTRODUCTION:
THE SEVEN WONDERS

TWO STATUES, a temple, a roof-top garden, two tombs and a lighthouse. This rather odd selection of seven monuments has become famous as the Seven Wonders of the Ancient World (Figure 1). Almost every schoolboy knows that such a list exists, but there are probably few people who could immediately name all seven, and there are even fewer who know anything about them or of how that list came to be chosen. Six of the seven have long been destroyed – some by the hand of nature and some desecrated by human hands. It is thus extremely difficult for us today to share the excitement that led to wonder amongst the people of ancient times.

Each of the chapters in this book describes one of the Seven Wonders and looks past the monument itself to the people responsible for the construction who had the vision to create something at which the whole world could marvel. Contemporary writings of those who knew and admired these Wonders help to underline that sense of awe which they engendered. Representations of them in sculptures and on coins depict them as they stood in the glory of their heyday, but it is only through the eyes of the archaeologists excavating at the very spot where the monuments once stood, and where now only fragmentary traces of their original grandeur remain, that they can live again – *sic transit gloria mundi*.

This is a journey back through time, to a world in which these monuments produced an immediate sense of wonder on the visitor. Only in this way is it possible to understand why these particular structures came to be chosen as the Seven Wonders of the World. The Epilogue of this book underlines that, from time to time, a number of other monuments from the ancient world have been included on the list, but never won universal approval. These, like the Seven Wonders themselves, stem from a variety of cultures and are a reminder of the ever-changing patterns of civilisation. Of one thing we may be sure: today's master-pieces will tomorrow be the fragmentary relics of the world that we know – the lesson of the Seven Wonders is a lesson for all time.

The Austrian architect Johann Fischer von Erlach (1656–1723) was one of the first to apply scientific research techniques to the study of ancient buildings. He opened his history of architecture in 1721 with the words:

> The chief aim of the author has been to show in a true light the most important of those famous monuments which the rust of time has devoured . . . and the reader may compare the Seven Wonders of the World as they are here depicted with other descriptions of them, which would surely not be recognized for what they were intended to be were it not for their names.

Two hundred and fifty years later the same sentiments apply. Today the list of the Seven Wonders is fixed for all time: the Pyramids, the Hanging Gardens, the statue of Olympian Zeus, the temple of Artemis, the Mausoleum, the Colossus and the Pharos. In the 1980s we know much, much more than von Erlach about the monuments and their creators. Yet a comprehensive account still requires to be written, to separate the facts from the fiction with which the post-Renaissance world has beguiled us.

The sites on which four of the monuments stood have now been excavated – Babylon in Iraq, Olympia in Greece, and Halicarnassus and Ephesos in Turkey. The pyramids at Giza in Egypt have been thoroughly explored. The writing of the ancient Babylonians and Egyptians in cuneiform and hieroglyphs can now be read and interpreted so that their history has been unfolded. Modern knowledge in detail of the whole of the ancient world has become so much more complete that a realistic picture of the Seven Wonders may now be drawn. The imaginative illustrations of Renaissance fantasy, however, still plague even recent accounts and continue to appear in textbooks. To discover the true picture that von Erlach would have desired, it is necessary to lift the veil placed over the monuments by our predecessors and, like him, to return to first principles. The originals must be reinspected from

1 *Map showing the locations of the Seven Wonders of the Ancient World and some other major sites*

ancient sources, the work of authors and artists who knew them as they stood, and the new evidence that has come to light through recent archaeological excavations must be properly sifted and assessed.

The origin of the Seven Wonders lies in people. Humans constantly survey their world and set beside the marvels of nature the works that have been imposed on the natural landscape by human hands. The question may not be asked consciously, but it lurks at the back of the sub-conscious: can mere man ever hope to equal the permanent majesty of snow-capped mountains or the tremendous power of the sea beating against cliffs in a gale-force

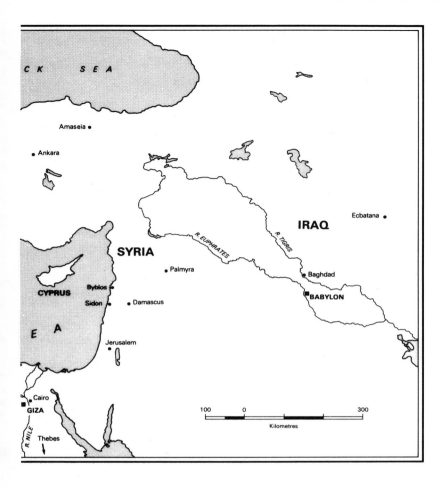

wind? Natural instincts led sailors to battle across oceans single-
handed against the elements, and make mountaineers overcome
the most difficult ascent in adverse conditions. So too architects
and sculptors are driven to express their visions in ways that have
never before been tried, to create monuments that will outlive not
only their creators, but even the very civilisations that gave them
birth. Above the black marble slab that covers the grave of Sir
Christopher Wren in the crypt of St. Paul's Cathedral is inscribed:
'*Si monumentum requiris, circumspice*' – if you seek his grave marker,
look around you. Wren's masterpiece was his tombstone. The
memorial of the Roman poet Horace was his poetry, 'more
timeless than bronze'. Such sentiments are echoed again and again
throughout the ages. It was the search to outlive the mortal limits

3

set upon us that was at the very root of the idea which could set aside seven great monuments to be named as the Seven Wonders of the World. Today man's ability to harness natural forces and to alter radically his natural environment give some semblance of immortality in overcoming the frailty of life's short span. The feelings of awe and pride in the most notable monuments of past and present naturally lead to wonder.

Yet it was not as 'wonders' that such monuments were first listed, but as 'sights' – not, in the Greek, *thaumata* (wonders), but as *theamata* (things to be seen), the dramatic monuments that fill the pages of modern guide books. As the 'sights' of the world came to be wondered at, so in common usage they became 'wonders'. *Theamata* made the simple linguistic change to *thaumata*. Succeeding generations considered the achievements of their predecessors and of their contemporaries, gradually evolving that select list of monuments that has today become fixed as the Seven Wonders of the World.

The number seven, 'lucky seven', like number three, indivisible, has assumed a role of importance through its use in magic and religious thought. It is unique in that it is neither a factor nor a product of any of the first ten numbers, a virgin number labelled by the Greek philosopher-mathematician Pythagoras and his followers with the name of the virgin goddess, Athena. Seven sets a limit, but is not in itself limiting. Perhaps more importantly, it allows an equality which prevents the one from being given precedence. A greater number would invite sub-division, encouraging, even demanding, that the objects on the list should be placed in order of importance. A lesser number would certainly force objects of equal merit to be excluded, creating a controversy of choice that might never be resolved. Beside the Seven Deadly Sins and the Seven Sages, the seven-branched candlestick (*menorah*) of the Temple at Jerusalem and the seven heavenly daughters of Atlas (seven stars named by the ancient Greeks the 'Pleiades') the list of the Seven Wonders of the World takes its place.

People of different ages and cultures have looked around them to select the very best monuments of their world for such a list and it is natural that, beside a kernel of undisputed masterpieces, a number of works should be included which did not win universal approval. It became necessary to select again from the many monuments that had been chosen by others to create a list that may be accepted as the canon. The list that we know today only became fixed in the Renaissance, at a time when scholars were looking back in admiration at the world of the Roman empire a thousand years before. At that distance they could discern with a dispassionate eye the monuments that had really made the greatest impact. The Dutch artist Maerten van Heemskerck (1498–1574) crystallised the ideas of his generation in a series of engravings which embody the now accepted list of monuments. It is perhaps only with the execution of these drawings that the list became fixed for all time, but the details of each monument have been scrutinised ever since under the scientific eye of such scholars as Johann Fischer von Erlach. The evidence on which van Heemskerck, von Erlach and their contemporaries drew lay in the literary sources surviving from the ancient world – the historians, orators and poets who, throughout the centuries of classical civilisation had looked at their own world and made their own selection. In the same way we too can look back at the ancient world to see how the idea of the Seven Wonders developed and blossomed until, today, it has become recognised and accepted by the whole of the western world, even to the extent of being featured in media advertisements.

The seeds for the list of the Seven Wonders were sown in the middle of the fifth century BC, in the *Histories* of Herodotus, often called the father of history. He was born about 484 BC in the city of Halicarnassus (modern Bodrum) on the south-west coast of Turkey, and he devoted his life to describing the clash of the two great civilisations of his day. In the east were the Persians, who had conquered the whole of the area in which Herodotus was born nearly a hundred years before. Around the basin of the Aegean Sea were the Greeks, many of them, like Herodotus himself, now subject to the Great King of Persia. The Greeks were concerned to ward off any attempt by the Persians to extend their empire westwards. In 480 BC the Greeks were victorious at the great sea-battle of Salamis. They drove back the expedition of the Persians led by Xerxes, the Great King, but only after Athens itself had been destroyed. Miraculously, the city, like the phoenix of legend, was born anew from the ashes, and the wonderful buildings now on the Acropolis arose from this very destruction.

Herodotus marvelled, as did many of his contemporaries, at the enormous achievements of the Persians and the great civilisations of the east. He was conscious of the importance of the Greek

2,3 *Maerten van Heemskerck's fanciful sixteenth-century representation of the pyramids of Egypt compared with the more accurate attempt by Fischer von Erlach in 1721*

victory over the greatest empire that the world had ever known, and he was also conscious of the new vision to be found in the blossoming of Greek civilisation. He found Babylon to be the most impressive of cities and became fascinated by the world of the Egyptians. Of all the monuments that he describes in his *Histories* it is the pyramids that receive his most devoted attention (Figures 2 and 3). At that time there was no question of there being a selection of Seven Wonders of the World. Indeed, Herodotus writing in the middle of the fifth century lived two hundred years before the construction of the latest of the monuments that now form the canonical list. He looked back into history, mesmerised by the achievements of the past which had survived into his own world. He looked around the world of his day, curious to study the effects of the past on the present and of

the present on the future. By a strange coincidence his birthplace, Halicarnassus, was itself to become a hundred years later the site of one of the monuments chosen for the Seven Wonders, the Mausoleum (Figures 4 and 5).

Herodotus leaves us in no doubt that of all the surviving relics of previous civilisations two stood out as truly remarkable in the fifth century BC – the great city of Babylon and the towering pyramids of Egypt. There is no suggestion that the Minoans and Mycenaeans, the Greeks' own ancestors in the Aegean world, had left any remains to match those of the Babylonians and Egyptians. When we analyse Herodotus' feelings, it is clear that sheer size played a major role in what impressed him. Standing in front of the pyramids at Giza he was overawed that mere humans could so match nature in creating mountains. It is the same with each of the Seven Wonders as the list became composed. It was size, majesty and beauty, all those qualities which produce a sense of awe, which in turn generated wonder. Size is in fact not a characteristic that might at once be connected with the greater master-pieces of the Greek world. There it is the refinement and close attention to detail which was the hallmark of such gems of

4,5 *The Mausoleum at Halicarnassus has been the subject of many reconstructions. Van Heemskerck's is more pictorial than von Erlach's architecturally balanced composition. There are still elements of the monument that spark discussion (see Figure 61)*

architecture as the Parthenon and the Erechtheion, created at Athens during Herodotus' lifetime. However, if much of what has survived of Greek civilisation is on a relatively small scale, there are plenty of monuments at which later generations could marvel, both for their size and for their remarkable attention to detail.

A hundred years after Herodotus, in 359 BC, Philip II ascended the throne of Macedonia. He used his military expertise to exercise his influence over the city states that divided up the country which we now know as Greece. At the time of his death in 336 BC Philip was preparing to launch an expedition to free the Greek cities of Asia Minor from Persian rule. Philip's son and successor, Alexander the Great, had the same vision as his father,

a united Greek world under Macedonian sovereignty. In 334 BC
Alexander led his army across the Hellespont, now called the
Dardanelles, the narrow strip of water that separates Europe from
Asia. This event changed the course of history. Alexander first
freed the Greek cities and then swept through the whole of the
Persian empire to India, to become himself King of Asia. His
successes changed the view that the Greeks had of themselves and
of their civilisation. The Greek world was now linked with that of
the east and a more universal view of human achievements was
evident. It was the watershed between the Hellenic and the
Hellenistic world and it was only after this that we find a list of
remarkable monuments being constructed, leading finally to the
choice of the Seven Wonders of the World.

The Greeks of the new world created by Alexander the Great
were able to compare it with the world of the past. The two
monuments that had so impressed themselves upon Herodotus,
the pyramids of Egypt and the city of Babylon, were still to be
seen dominating the architecture of the now far-flung Macedonian
empire. At Babylon there were two structures which had no
parallel elsewhere, and it is not surprising that the gigantic walls

surrounding the city and the fascinating Hanging Gardens found a place in the early lists of monuments (Figure 6).

Looking at the more recent past, at the 'classical' Greek world of the fifth and fourth centuries BC, before the Macedonian conquest of the east, one massive temple stood out above all others – that of Artemis at Ephesos, where in Roman times the great goddess Diana of the Ephesians was worshipped. The Greeks could also point to the enormous statue of Zeus at Olympia and to the great tomb of Maussollos, the vassal of the Persians, at Halicarnassus, as monuments that far surpassed others in scale and execution. These had survived from earlier generations and each had the qualities which produced a sense of awe in the onlooker. They gave to their creators that immortality which is so sought after by every generation.

6 *The phenomenal walls of Babylon dominate the foreground of Maerten van Heemskerck's reconstruction and the Hanging Gardens take second place in the background, right*

7 *Both Johann von Ehrlach and Maerten van Heemskerck (see Figure 67) were agreed that the Colossus of Rhodes bestrode the harbour entrance, as Shakespeare would have us believe. This would have been technically impossible in terms of ancient bronze-casting*

The two latest monuments to be accepted into the canon of the Seven Wonders give a clue to the date at which such a list could have been compiled. The earlier of the two was the Colossus, the statue of the sun-god Helios which stood at the entrance to the harbour of the city of Rhodes (Figure 7). This was constructed as a thank-offering to the god in commemoration of his help in successfully withstanding the long siege of Rhodes by Macedonian forces in 305 BC. The statue was probably completed well before 250 BC. The last of the Seven Wonders, and one that does not appear in lists of such monuments for nearly a thousand years, was the great lighthouse at Alexandria in Egypt, the Pharos, which gave its name to all lighthouses in the Greek world. This was erected during the reign of Ptolemy II Philadelphus (284–246 BC). His kingdom had been carved from the Macedonian empire by his father, Ptolemy I, after Alexander's death.

The Colossus of Rhodes hardly survived the completion of the Pharos. In 226 BC a terrible earthquake at Rhodes threw down the statue and, despite the Rhodians' longing to have it set up again, it lay where it had fallen for many centuries. It was there for all to see but, however great the achievement in erecting the statue, the sad heap of broken bronze would hardly qualify the Colossus to be listed among the seven most admired works of mankind. Although, therefore, the list was not finally crystallised until the Renaissance, by which time so many of the monuments had crumbled to dust, the thirty-year period between the construction of the Pharos and the destruction of the Colossus must be regarded as a period of vital importance in the creation of the idea of the Seven Wonders. At that very time, Callimachus of Cyrene (305–240 BC), who held an important post in the Library at Alexandria in Egypt, wrote a work entitled 'A collection of wonders in lands throughout the world'. This has not survived, nor are its contents known in any detail, but the existence of such a collection must certainly have hastened the selection of a few, leading ultimately to the choice of the Seven Wonders themselves. The first list of seven such monuments occurs in a short poem attributed to Antipater, a Greek poet from Sidon on the Palestinian coast, just over a hundred years after the death of Callimachus. The poem is a simple statement of admiration for these great human achievements:

> I have gazed on the walls of impregnable Babylon, along which chariots may race, and on the Zeus by the banks of the Alphaeus. I have seen the Hanging Gardens and the Colossus of Helios, the great man-made mountains of the lofty pyramids, and the gigantic tomb of Maussollos. But when I saw the sacred house of Artemis that towers to the clouds, the others were placed in the shade, for the sun himself has never looked upon its equal outside Olympus.

The walls and Hanging Gardens of Babylon, the pyramids of Egypt, the statue of Zeus at Olympia, the Colossus of Rhodes, the tomb of Maussollos, and the temple of Artemis at Ephesos. This list is close enough to the Seven Wonders as we know them today to provide the evidence that the idea of the Seven Wonders may be traced back to the second century BC.

THE GREAT PYRAMID
OF GIZA

PETER A. CLAYTON

THE PYRAMIDS of Egypt have always been listed from the beginning amongst the Seven Wonders of the Ancient World, but it is actually the Great Pyramid at Giza that is the focus of attention and takes its place at the head of the list. It is the only one of the Seven Wonders that still stands in an almost complete and recognisable form; it is also the oldest. Built for the pharaoh Khufu (or Cheops, as the Greek historian Manetho calls him) of the Fourth Dynasty, about 2560 BC, the pyramid represents the high water mark of pyramid building in Old Kingdom Egypt.

The Greek priest/historian Manetho, who came from Sebennytus in the Delta of Egypt, wrote a history of Egypt during the reign of Ptolemy II (284–246 BC). In it he divided ancient Egyptian history into a series of thirty dynasties. These fell into three main sections – the Old Kingdom (First to Sixth Dynasties, c. 3100–2181 BC, although the first three dynasties are also referred to as the Archaic period); the Middle Kingdom (Eleventh and Twelfth Dynasties, c. 2133–1786 BC), and the New Kingdom (Eighteenth to Twentieth Dynasties, c. 1567–1085 BC). These represented periods of central government stability (ma'at in ancient Egyptian, a goddess represented by the Feather of Truth who governed all things that the Egyptian relied upon – truth, stability, the never-changing cycle of life, etc.). In between these three major periods were times of instability with the breakdown of central government. They are known respectively as the First Intermediate Period (Seventh to Tenth Dynasties, c. 2181–c. 2133 BC), and the Second Intermediate Period (Thirteenth to Seventeenth Dynasties, c. 1786–1567 BC). It was during the latter period that Egypt first suffered domination by outside peoples, the Hyksos (the so-called 'Shepherd Kings') who came from the Syria/Palestine area and were finally expelled in the mid-sixteenth century BC by warlike princes of Thebes in Upper Egypt who founded the Eighteenth Dynasty and the New Kingdom. Egyptologists refer to the period after the Twentieth Dynasty either as the Third Intermediate Period or the Late Period (c. 1085–343 BC). This includes the Twenty-sixth or Saite Dynasty (664–525 BC), a period of renaissance of Egyptian art and architecture. The Twenty-seventh Dynasty (525–404 BC) had seen Egypt ruled by Persia with a resurgence in the Twenty-eighth to Thirtieth Dynasties. After the death of Nectanebo II, the last native pharaoh, in 343 BC Egypt was once again ruled by Persia and then, with the coming of Alexander the Great in 332 BC, by the Macedonian Greeks. They ruled as the Ptolemaic dynasty until the suicide of the last of the line, Cleopatra VII, in 30 BC when Egypt became a Roman province.

The building of pyramids is essentially an ancient Egyptian phenomenon although there are pyramidal structures elsewhere, notably in the New World but the latter served different functions, had a different shape and the earliest were built at least 1000 years after the last Egyptian royal pyramid. Cheops' pyramid (to use the generally better known Greek form of his name) is not an isolated phenomenon but the apogee of a long line of tomb development that culminates at Giza and which then deteriorates thereafter. The Pyramids of the Fifth and Sixth Dynasties are sorry affairs and the last royal examples of the Eleventh and Twelfth Dynasties not much better. Subsequently the royal burials during the New Kingdom were made at the religious capital, Thebes (modern Luxor) in Upper Egypt. They were hidden in the Valley of the Kings on the west bank, a remote valley still under the guardianship of a pyramid, a natural one known as the 'Lady of the Peak', which rises high above the valley and is sacred to the goddess Meretseger, 'she who loves silence'.

Pyramids are the very epitome of kingship in ancient Egypt but, although large royal tombs, they have a long line of antecedents that stretch back to the small royal tombs of the earliest dynasties. There is an architectural progression to be observed which culminates in the Great Pyramid. The royal tombs of the first two dynasties, c. 3100–c. 2686 BC, are still a matter of some debate amongst Egyptologists as to whether they are located at Abydos, a site in Upper Egypt sacred to Osiris, the god of the dead, or at Saqqara, the necropolis of Memphis, the ancient capital of Egypt, which lies just south of modern Cairo. The problem lies in the fact that two tombs were prepared, one as the actual tomb and the other as a cenotaph. In this double provision the old title of pharaoh since the unification of Upper and Lower Egypt under Menes (or Narmer) in *c.* 3100 BC was fulfilled: 'King of Upper and Lower Egypt, Lord of the Two Lands', and he had a burial place in each area. Due first to the ravages of the early tomb robbers and then of time, it has proved very difficult for the main excavators of these two sites, Sir Flinders Petrie and Professor W.B. Emery respectively, to settle the question finally. Often the only remaining inscribed evidence amongst the debris consists of clay wine-jar seals, the rest is of broken pottery and what the robbers discarded as useless. These 'rejects' give us but a glimpse of the splendid furniture of carved wood and ivory, beautifully studied animals such as lions and lionesses in ivory, coursing hounds, etc., which were used as gaming pieces, and the like that were placed in the rooms adjoining the main burial chamber.

Two different forms of monument are evident at Abydos and Saqqara. At Abydos the burial chamber and its attendant storerooms were dug underground and roofed with timber baulks buried beneath a low mound. At Saqqara similar provision was made but the superstructure of the tomb took the form of a 'mastaba' (so-called by the Arabs because it resembled the bench outside the door of native houses). This low, flat-topped structure had an ornamental façade around it; known as the 'palace' façade. It consisted of alternate pilasters and alcoves of mud brick forming an articulated wall. At Saqqara, Emery found the two kinds of superstructure together in the tomb of Queen Herneit, the tumulus pyramid directly over the burial with the surrounding 'palace' façade walls. He considered this to be a prototype for the later royal tomb, the Step Pyramid of King Zoser of the Third Dynasty (less than a mile away in the necropolis). For the nobility in the Old Kingdom the mastaba tomb became the standard type of burial but for the pharaoh it developed. Zoser, the third king of the Third Dynasty, *c.* 2670 BC, had his monument built at Saqqara by his vizier and architect Imhotep (who was deified in the Late Period as a god of medicine and architecture). Imhotep introduced an innovation: he built in stone, using small blocks, for the first time in history. Zoser's tomb, the Step Pyramid, began life as a normal mastaba but was enlarged three times, in reality becoming three mastabas placed one upon the other and culminating in a structure some 70m (204ft) high and having seven steps. This is the first pyramid, but it was not a true pyramid since the sides, the 'steps', were not filled in to produce a smooth outer surface. Zoser's successor, Sekhemkhet, had his tomb built nearby and, although unfinished, we know that it followed the same style. Huni, the last king of the Third Dynasty, c. 2615 BC, built his pyramid at Meydum, to the south of Saqqara. This was begun as a step pyramid but the steps were filled in to give a smooth outer casing. There seems to have been a problem with this since the pyramid suffered a collapse at some point that left it with its present curious, almost lighthouse (pharos), shape.

At the beginning of the Fourth Dynasty Sneferu, the first king, began building his tomb in what is the more accepted pyramid shape. In fact, he had two pyramids, both at Dahshur and about a mile apart. The earlier of the two is known as the Bent or Rhomboid Pyramid because it suddenly changes its angle from a slope of 54 degrees to 42½ degrees. The late Professor Kurt Mendelssohn suggested that the pyramids at Meydum and Dahshur were built concurrently, not consecutively, and that there was a sudden disaster, a collapse, at Meydum, perhaps after a heavy downpour of rain. The architect working at Dahshur probably thought that the angle of the slope of the pyramid's outer face was a contributing factor and accordingly cut it at Dahshur to give the Bent Pyramid its shape. The other pyramid of Sneferu, the Northern Pyramid, a mile away, has an angle of 43 degrees 36 minutes, much shallower than its predecessors but one that is closer to the eventual accepted slope.

These then are the antecedents of Cheops' pyramid at Giza. Cheops was the son of Sneferu and must have been very familiar with the architectural as well as the logistical problems involved with his father's tomb. The pyramid shape itself was closely tied up with the worship of the sun-god Re of Heliopolis. It began as the stubby obelisk upon which the benu bird alighted in the creation myths and also represented the culmination of the sun's rays as they reached down to earth – a natural phenomenon that can still be observed in the right weather conditions. When Cheops began the construction of his pyramid at Giza he therefore had a religious background as well as a long evolution as guidance.

In 1974 Professor Mendelssohn published two interesting theories: one was that the Meydum pyramid collapse influenced the building changes evident at Dahshur; the other, closely allied with this, was that not all the pyramids in the Old Kingdom were built consecutively, i.e. one after the other as required by each pharaoh for his burial, but concurrently, i.e. more than one might be in process of building at the same time, which would explain Meydum and Dahshur. As a corollary to this he added a further observation — there are more pyramids extant in the Old Kingdom than there are known pharaohs. Some of the pyramids do not appear to have been used for a burial; for example, at Meydum the burial chamber is very small and also unfinished, and there is no trace of a sarcophagus ever having been in it. At Dahshur Sneferu could only have been buried in one of the two pyramids. Mendelssohn therefore put forward the radical suggestion that pyramid-building was not due solely to religious motivation but that it also had another function, to be a great national endeavour which thus gave cohesion to the growing state of Egypt. His suggestions, it must be admitted, have not found favour with all the Egyptological fraternity, but they did at least highlight a number of problems and should not be too lightly dismissed.

With Huni, the last king of the Third Dynasty, another innovation appears at Meydum connected with the pyramid. We see the beginnings of the 'pyramid complex', the pyramid being part of a set arrangement along with other buildings. (At Saqqara the Step Pyramid had been set within a large enclosure with associated dummy buildings.) The pyramid funerary complex consisted of four parts. It began with a Valley Temple built on the edge of the cultivation. Here the pharaoh's embalmed body would be brought across the Nile from the embalmers' quarters for burial. From the Valley Temple a long Causeway led up to the site of the pyramid. Initially the Causeway was used as a roadway to transport the huge blocks of stone brought by barge on the Nile flood to the Valley Temple site. When that aspect of the pyramid construction was complete the Causeway took on a religious connotation. Its sides were built up, decorated with sculpted scenes (as we can see in the reconstructed section of the Fifth Dynasty Causeway of the pharaoh Unas at Saqqara) and

17

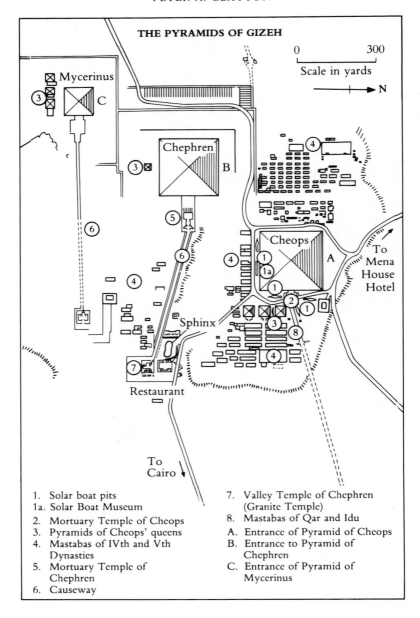

8 Site plan of the pyramid complex at Giza. (Courtesy of Swan Hellenic Ltd)

9 *Seated statute of the Vizier Hemon,' cousin of Cheops and chief-of-works for the Great Pyramid. Height 1.56m. (Pelizaeus Museum, Hildersheim, Germany)*

roofed over with just a narrow slit left to admit some light. Up this enclosed route the pharaoh's body would be brought, safe from impious eyes, to the Mortuary or Pyramid Temple that was built at its end against the east face of the pyramid. From here, after the appropriate rituals, the mummy would be taken round the side of the pyramid to the entrance on the north face and thence into the interior to the burial chamber. At the Great Pyramid the Mortuary Temple still stands, but very much ruined, against the platform on the east face. The Causeway can be picked out on the surface but the Valley Temple has not been excavated and lies beneath the modern Arab village to the east on the edge of the cultivation.

Cheops chose a new site for his tomb, the edge of the Libyan desert on the plateau at Giza. He was to be followed here by at least two of his major successors in the Fourth Dynasty: Chephren (Khafra), and Mykerinus (Menkaura) (Figure 8). We believe that his architect, or more properly his chief-of-works, was his cousin the Vizier Hemon, whose seated statue was found in a tomb at Giza in the last century and is now in the Pelizaeus Museum,

10 *Tiny ivory statuette of Cheops, seated holding the flail in his right hand and wearing the Red Crown of Lower Egypt. His name is inscribed in a serekh on the side of the throne beside his right leg. Found at Abydos. (Cairo Museum)*

Hildersheim, West Germany (Figure 9). It shows a powerfully built man, corpulent in the manner of Old Kingdom sculpture to show a person of position and eminence. Most statue representations tend to be rather idealised, showing the subject in the prime of life. With Hemon, the facial features have been damaged by tomb robbers who prised out the inlaid eyes that gave it a lifelike appearance. This effect was achieved by using obsidian and crystal as the pupils, white limestone for the irises and the whole set within a bronze surround.

Curiously, despite all the size and importance of the Great Pyramid, there is only one surviving complete representation of its builder Cheops. This is a tiny ivory statuette of the king found in 1903 by Petrie in the foundations of the Osiris temple at Abydos (Figure 10). The king is seen seated holding a flail in his right hand and wearing the Red Crown of Lower Egypt. On the front of the throne on which he sits is inscribed his name, enclosed in the royal serekh. Despite its diminutive size and the material, it is a portrait with strong characteristics. There are some superb portraits of the other builders at Giza, notably the seated diorite statue of Chephren and the series of slate triad plaques, as well as statues, of Mykerinus.

Before building work could commence it was necessary to prepare the site – it had to be made level and also the proposed sides had to be carefully oriented with the four cardinal points of the compass. The levelling was probably done by marking out the appropriate area with a series of four low mud walls. The enclosure formed was then filled with water. Naturally, the surface of the water would be level. A series of trenches would be cut into the bed-rock in such a way that their bottoms were at a constant level beneath the water surface. When sufficient had been cut to cover adequately the area under consideration, the water would be run off and the rock between the trenches cut away, thus providing a level surface. There was a slight exception in the case of the Great Pyramid. In the centre of the proposed building area an outcrop of natural rock was left. How large this was is not known, although parts of it can be seen within the makeup of the integral passageways of the pyramid.

The exact orientation of the sides of the pyramid had to be obtained by observation of the stars, since no compass was known at the time. How accurate the ancient Egyptians were may be judged by the fact that the error of alignment on the four sides is only a matter of fractions of a degree. The difference in length between the longest and shortest of the four square sides is less than 20cm (7.9 in). This latter is quite incredible when two things are considered in relation to the Great Pyramid: first, all measurements had to be along the sides, it was not possible to carry out diagonal checks across the middle because of the knoll of rock left there; and, second, all these measurements were carried out with ropes or cords made of palm or flax-fibre, which must have been subject to stretching.

Once these initial preparations were complete building work could begin in earnest, and with it a number of problems that still puzzle Egyptologists today. Despite the solid evidence of the pyramid itself, standing high above Cairo on the Giza plateau, and the numerous theories put forward, it is not known exactly how the pyramid was built. It has to be remembered that the ancient Egyptians did not have the knowledge of the pulley, or the block and tackle, until the Roman period, two and half thousand years after the Great Pyramid was built. The only 'mechanical' assistance available was the use of rollers and levers. By these two very primitive means all buildings, statues and obelisks were erected or moved in ancient Egypt.

There are two major theories as to how the pyramids were built: one, using ramps that encircled the building as it rose, the other involving a long building ramp stretching out into the desert, heightened and lengthened as necessary with the rise of the pyramid. Neither is a totally satisfactory explanation. A third alternative that might spring to mind is the use of scaffolding, possibly raising the blocks on cradles, as the lintels wre raised to form the trilithons at Stonehenge. This is not feasible on two counts: wood was at a premium in ancient Egypt, none of suitable calibre for this use existed and the quantities required would have been enormous; also, the vast size, and more especially the weight of the blocks (five tons is amongst the lightest), would have made this impractical.

The encircling ramp idea has a lot to commend it. Ramps of mud brick would rise around each of the four sides of the pyramid as it progressed, the huge blocks being brought up on rollers. As the block passed over the back roller it was freed and would be replaced at the front and the block hauled forward by gangs of men on ropes. It all presents a very feasible, theoretical picture (and there is a good model of this method in the Museum of Science, Boston), but the practicalities leave much to be desired. A shallow slope, necessitated by the weight of the blocks, rising around all sides would create two major problems: the first, that of the gangs negotiating the corners and keeping the block balanced on the rollers under control. The second is the problem of moving the blocks up and up and round and round the structure eventually to reach the upper levels. This would involve an inordinate amount of labour and control over many gangs moving blocks at the various levels on the way up the slopes. The sheer flow of humanity up and down the ramps would be incredible.

The external ramp theory proposed by that doyen of French Egyptologists, Jean-Philippe Lauer, is also interesting but, similarly, has its problems. Lauer suggested a single ramp that was extended and heightened as appropriate to the height that the pyramid had reached. This sounds perfectly feasible, until some mathematical calculations are made. The steepest slope upon which it is possible to manoeuvre a five-ton block on rollers is 1 in 10. To finish the upper courses of the pyramid would require a ramp stretching one mile out into the desert and rising eventually to a height above that of the dome of St Paul's Cathedral. It is interesting to reflect that until the nineteenth century AD the Great Pyramid was the tallest man-made building in the world – it held its record for over four thousand years without the aid of modern technology!

There is a third theory extant as to how the Great Pyramid was built. It was put forward by Peter Hodges, an English Master Builder, who took a very practical interest in the problems of moving horizontally and lifting huge weights with only rollers and levers at one's disposal. Working in his yard with a two-ton test load he was able to demonstrate that two men could move this quite easily by making use of long levers that had a short angled foot at one end protected by a metal shoe. By inserting this end beneath the block in pairs, or more depending on its size, one end of the block could be raised and packing placed beneath it. The process would be repeated at the other end and the movement continued upwards by use of such packing and blocks. Thus a large block could be raised relatively easily to a reasonable height. The construction of the pyramid was in levels, each 'step' being quite broad and on average not much more than a metre in height. Hodges's principle would allow groups of workers raising blocks on all four faces at once and also several groups along the length of each face, lessening in numbers as the sides became shorter the higher the pyramid rose. As each block reached its appropriate level it would be moved across the surface on rollers in the normal way to its allotted place. The method has much to commend it, especially as it does appear to overcome several of the basic problems of logistics in the construction. In connection with this proposal it is interesting to note that Herodotus, in Book 2 of his *History* says,

After laying the stones for the base, they raised the remaining stones to their places by means of machines formed of short wooden planks. The first machine raised them from the ground to the top of the first step. On this there was another machine, which received the stone upon its arrival, and conveyed it to the second step, whence a third machine advanced it still higher.

Once the basic construction was finished the pyramid had to be cased in blocks of gleaming white Tura limestone quarried from the Moqqatam Hills just to the east of modern Cairo. The casing was effected from the apex downwards, blocks of limestone being set on the 'steps' and filling them in, then cut and smoothed down to achieve the appropriate angle and gleaming appearance. All the pyramids (except the Step Pyramid) were cased. The Blunt Pyramid at Dahshur retains most of its outer casing because it was set into the body of the pyramid at an angle, thereby held in place by the weight of the blocks above, and consequently difficult to remove at a later date for other purposes. At Giza, Chephren's pyramid still retains some of its limestone casing high up at the apex, but the rest has gone, as it has from the pyramids of Cheops and Mykerinus, largely to be used in the building of medieval Cairo.

Before proceeding further and describing the internal arrangements of the Great Pyramid it might be appropriate at this point to present its essential dimensions (Figure 11). The angle of the slope of the sides was 54 degrees 54 minutes, which became the norm for subsequent Egyptian pyramids. Its height was 145.75m (481ft), but it has lost its top 10m (30ft) and is actually truncated

11 *The Great Pyramid of Cheops seen from the south-west. In front of the south face is the boat-shaped museum that now houses Cheops' boat*

although at a distance neither the lack of its casing nor of its apex is really noticeable. The sides are 229m square (756ft) with less than 20cm (7.9 inches) difference between the longest and shortest sides. It covers an area of 5.37 ha (13.1 acres), which, it has been calculated, can accommodate St Peter's Rome, with the cathedrals of Florence and Milan, plus Westminster Abbey and St Paul's London. It is difficult to calculate the number of blocks used because of the unknown quantity of the mass of natural rock in the centre, but figures of 2,300,000 separate blocks of between 2 and 15 tons each have been quoted.

It was part of the religious requirements in the Old Kingdom that the entrance to the pyramid should be located on the north side, facing the polar stars. All conform to this, the only variation being the Second Pyramid at Giza (Chephren's) which has two entrances on the north, one slightly off centre some 10m high up the face of the pyramid and the other almost directly below it in the surrounding pavement. The only exception is the Blunt Pyramid at Dahshur, which has a second entrance high up on the western face, as well as the statutory one in the north face. Cheops is no exception and has a low entrance about 17m (55 ft) up its north face and 7.5m (24 ft) east of the central point. This has four large blocks, in two pairs, set pyramidically above it to help relieve the pressure from the blocks above (Figure 12). The modern entrance to the pyramid is just below the original one and a little to the right of it. This was made in the ninth century, according to Muslim tradition, by the Caliph Ma'mun, the son of the famous Haroun al-Rashid, well known from the stories of the One Thousand and One Nights (the Arabian Nights). It is known as 'Ma'mun's Hole' and was made when he searched in vain for an entrance to retrieve the treasure that legend said was still within. The Arab accounts speak of a great golden cockerel and an emerald the size of a roc's egg being found, but the reality of our knowledge about Old Kingdom royal burial provision denies this. The tomb robbers of ancient Egypt had been too thorough when they broke into and robbed the pyramid, probably during the collapse of central government in the First Intermediate Period (the Seventh to Tenth Dynasties).

Examination of the section of the Great Pyramid immediately shows that it was subject to at least three changes of plan during its building (Figure 13). It has more internal passages and chambers than any of the other Old Kingdom pyramids. The

12 *The ancient entrance, above, to the Great Pyramid on the north face and, slightly below to the right, the modern entrance forced by the Caliph Ma'mun and now that used by tourists*

initial plan seems to have been for a descending passageway from the entrance leading to a burial chamber located in the centre and below ground level, a plan previously seen at Meydum and both Dahshur pyramids and which Chephren was to follow later. However, this chamber remained unfinished and an alternative rising passage (the Ascending Corridor) was made which led to a chamber located higher up in the body of the pyramid and more central under the apex. This also remained unfinished and today is known colloquially and inaccurately as the 'Queen's Chamber'. The third change in plan involved a much more grandiose scheme. It began with a new gallery being built rising up into the heart of the pyramid from the end of the Ascending Corridor and its junction with the passage leading to the 'Queen's Chamber'. This is known as the Grand Gallery, which indeed it is in all respects. It is 47m long (153 ft) and 8.5m (28 ft) high. Its polished limestone walls rise vertically for two metres and then the next seven courses move gradually inwards to form a corbelled vault that is truly amazing and unparalleled in Old Kingdom architecture (Figure 14). It is eventually roofed by a single slab of stone

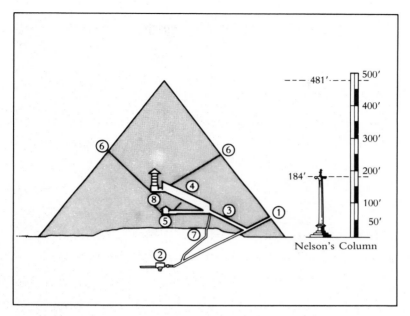

13 *Cross-section of the Great Pyramid looking west. 1 The entrance on the north face and the descending corridor. 2 The unfinished chamber intended originally to be the burial chamber. 3 Ascending Corridor. 4 Grand Gallery. 5 'Queen's Chamber'. 6 Air shafts leading from the King's Chamber to the outer surface of the pyramid. 7 Escape shaft used by the workmen after the burial was completed. 8 Burial Chamber, the King' Chamber. Nelson's Column, Trafalgar Square, London, is shown for comparison in height*

just over a metre in width. The Grand Gallery was to serve a secondary purpose, as we shall see shortly.

At the head of the Grand Gallery there is a short, low passageway that has three slots cut into its roof that once held portcullises of granite to be lowered into place and block the entrance to the passage and the burial chamber beyond. This low passage leads into the north-east corner of the burial chamber, the King's Chamber. It is constructed of huge blocks of polished granite and its shape is the 'golden mean' of 2:1 – 10.58m by 5.29m (34 ft 4 ins by 17 ft 2 ins). It is 5.87m high (19 ft 1 in.) to its flat roof which consists of nine huge blocks that weigh in total around 400 tons. Above the King's Chamber roof is a series of five 'relieving' chambers, all with flat roofs except the highest,

15 *The black granite sarcophagus at the west end of the King's Chamber*

which is pitched. The blocks involved here are rough-finished as they came from the quarry and several still carry their quarry marks painted in red ochre, including the name of Cheops – the only instance where it occurs in the pyramid.

At the west end of the burial chamber, standing flush on the floor and a little way out from the wall, is a large black granite sarcophagus, now lidless and with a large section missing from the upper south-east corner (Figure 15). It was cut and hollowed from a single block of granite and the saw marks may still be seen on it. Despite the break in its corner it still 'rings' with a bell-like sound when struck, even with the heel of the hand. When Petrie surveyed the pyramid in 1880–2 he found that the sarcophagus was about 2.5cm (one inch) wider than the entrance to the Ascending Corridor. It therefore could not have been introduced

14 *Looking up the Grand Gallery in the Great Pyramid to the top where the strip light marks the entrance to the passageway leading to the King's Chamber. Note the slots for timber baulks in the side ledges and the way in which the wall blocks move forward over each other ultimately to form a corbel roof*

29

into the burial chamber through the corridor but must have been put into place as the pyramid was being built, before a roof was placed on the King's Chamber. It really qualifies as being the first example of 'built in' furniture in the world.

Other features of the burial chamber are the two small 'air shafts' that occur in the north and south walls, starting about a metre above the floor and passing through the bulk of the pyramid to the outer surface. Their exact purpose is not known although it has been suggested that they were originally oriented with the polar stars, an essential aspect of Old Kingdom religion, and, since they no longer do so, the earth's axis must have changed since the pyramid was built. This is not capable of being astronomically proved and their actual function is still not known.

It was mentioned earlier that the Grand Gallery also served a second function. It was the place where the great blocking plugs of granite were stored which were used to seal the Ascending Corridor after the burial had occurred. They were too big to be accommodated anywhere else in the area. The evidence is that they were supported on cross beams of wood sufficiently above the floor of the Gallery for the funerary cortege to move beneath them at the time of the burial. Subsequently, the priests retreated and left behind a gang of workmen who proceeded to knock the baulks away and let the granite plugs fall and slide down to block the Ascending Corridor. In so doing, of course, they were themselves trapped behind the plugs in the interior of the pyramid, on the side of the burial. They had, however, an escape route, since it was not the practice to inter the workforce in the Old Kingdom. Their escape route was via a narrow shaft that led from beneath a stone in the upper corridor at the top of the Grand Gallery, down through the body of the pyramid to emerge below the lower corridor. This they escaped by, blocking behind them both it and then the passageway to the outer face and the entrance. Despite all these precautions the pyramid was still robbed in antiquity, probably around the twenty-third century BC. The pyramid was open in late antiquity, as we can learn from the accounts of classical writers, but then the entrance was once more lost under debris so that Ma'mun had to make a forced entry in the ninth century AD.

The Great Pyramid was already two thousand years old when Herodotus of Halicarnassus, the 'father of history', visited Egypt in the mid-fifth century BC. He wrote a description of many of the ancient monuments, some from actual personal observation, others from second-hand accounts that he was given. In Book 2 of his *History* he treats Egypt in some detail. Of the Great Pyramid he wrote:

> There is an inscription in Egyptian characters on the pyramid which records the quantity of radishes, onions and garlic consumed by the labourers who constructed it; and I perfectly well remember that the interpreter who read the writing to me said that the money expended in this way was 1600 talents of silver [just over £5 million at present silver prices]. If this then is a true record, what a vast sum must have been spent on the iron tools [sic.: there was little if no iron in Egypt before the Eighteenth Dynasty (an iron-bladed dagger and a few minor amulets found in the tomb of Tutankhamen) until the Roman period], used in the work, and on the feeding and clothing of the labourers, considering the length of time the work lasted.

Herodotus says that it took ten years to build the causeway and twenty to build the pyramid. A workforce of 100,000 men was employed. As far as we know, Cheops actually reigned about 23 years. Obviously in certain respects Herodotus was a little gullible in recording all that he was told, but then today many of the dragomen that frequent the Giza plateau are equally prepared to spin similar stories to the incredulous tourist.

Diodorus Siculus (*fl.* 60–30 BC) observed in his *Library of History* (Book 1, 63):

> The eighth king, Chemmis [i.e. Cheops/Khufu] of Memphis ruled 50 years and constructed the largest of the three pyramids, which are numbered amongst the seven wonders of the world. These pyramids, which are situated on the side of Egypt which is toward Libya, are 120 stadia [about 13½ miles] from Memphis and 45 stadia [five miles] from the Nile, and by the immensity of their structures and the skill shown in their execution they fill the beholder with wonder and astonishment.
>   . . . for though no fewer than a thousand years have elapsed, as they say, or, some writers have it, more than 3,400, the stones remain to this day still preserving their original position and the entire structure undecayed.

He says that 360,000 men were employed and the project was completed in 20 years.

Strabo (*c.* 64 BC–AD 21) is able to add some points in his *Geography* (Book 17, 33):

> the tombs of the kings, of which three are noteworthy; and two of these are even numbered amongst the Seven Wonders of the World, for they are a stadium in height [about 202 yards] . . . one of them is only a little larger than the other. High up, approximately midway between the sides, it has a movable stone, and when this is raised up there is a sloping passage to the vault.

Of particular interest is his reference to a flap door that could be raised. Presumably the original entrance through the Tura limestone casing was disguised to blend with the rest of the casing and could well have been such a door. At the time the classical authors saw the pyramid it still had its casing substantially intact; it was only removed some centuries after them for re-use in the building of medieval Cairo.

The Great Pyramid and its two later major companions dominated the skyline at the edge of the Libyan desert. They each had official names when they were constructed – 'Cheops is one belonging to the Horizon', 'Great is Chephren', and 'Mykerinus is divine'. Ever since classical times it was believed that the Second Pyramid, of Chephren, was a solid structure with no internal arrangements. This was disproved on 2 March 1818 when the Italian Egyptologist Giovanni Battista Belzoni found the upper entrance on the north face and penetrated to the burial chamber which, needless to say, had been robbed in early antiquity. The Third Pyramid, of Mykerinus, was explored by Colonel Howard Vyse and John Perring in the 1830s and they found a sarcophagus decorated with the 'palace façade' (the only decorated sarcophagus in the three pyramids of Giza). This was subsequently lost at sea when the ship carrying it to England foundered after leaving Leghorn. A wooden anthropoid coffin found at the same time, not the original coffin but a later, Saite, pious restoration (which the sarcophagus may also have been), travelled separately and is now in the British Museum.

The pyramids of Giza have always excited the interest and curiosity of humankind by their very size, solidity and, almost, aloofness. Often called the 'Mountains of Pharaoh' they have also been referred to as the 'Granaries of Joseph'. At one time in the medieval period they were seriously thought of as having a

16 *French bronze medallion commemorating the Battle of the Pyramids on 21 July 1798 (the date of 25 July on the medallion is incorrect). Napoleon is seen exhorting his troops before they engage the Mamelukes. (Author's collection)*

connection with Joseph although, as we now know, their internal arrangements would certainly not have been conducive to storing enough grain to alleviate the seven years of famine.

With the French invasion of Egypt in 1798 the pyramids of Giza once more entered the stage of history. On 21 July the French army inflicted a crushing defeat on the Mamelukes outside Cairo. It is always referred to as the Battle of the Pyramids, but the actual field of battle was some ten miles away at Embaba. Lejeune's famous painting at Versailles correctly shows the pyramids on the far horizon. The French medallions commemorating the battle show Napoleon haranguing his troops before the onslaught, either standing or on horseback, in the pyramids' shadow (Figure 16). Intuitively his exhortation to the troops, recorded on the medallions, runs: 'Soldats! Du haute de ces pyramides 40 siècles nous contemplent' – 'Soldiers, from the height of these pyramids forty centuries are watching us'. He had a sense of history and made an inspired guess since at the time no one had any idea how old the pyramids were – 'forty centuries', four thousand years, gives a date around 2,200 BC and the Great Pyramid was built about 2,560 BC. After the victory, the story goes, Napoleon sat and rested in the shade at the base of the Great Pyramid whilst some of his more active young officers climbed to the top. Upon their return he greeted them with the information that he had calculated there was enough stone in the three pyramids to build a wall 3 metres (10 feet) high and 30 centimetres thick (a foot) around France. This was apparently subsequently confirmed by the mathematician Monge who was present in the party of savants under the direction of the Baron Vivant Denon.

For many on the fringe of Egyptological studies the Great Pyramid has had a totally different aspect other than being the tomb of the pharaoh. To their mind it is a key to the past and future history of the world, a secret which is hidden from the generality in the mystic 'pyramid inch', a specific length of the ancient Egyptian measure, the cubit. The father of these outlandish theories was Charles Piazzi Smyth, one-time Astronomer Royal of Scotland, who surveyed the pyramid and published his theories in *Our Inheritance in the Great Pyramid* (1864). In essence, he suggests that certain measurements taken from the pyramid, when divided by the 'pyramid inch' or 'royal cubit' gave historical dates back before the pyramid's construction and also forward in that it could foretell events millennia ahead. Two examples will suffice to illustrate this. First, if the line of the outer casing is projected downwards in theory below the ground level, and also similarly the line of the Ascending Corridor, they will eventually meet. That distance, divided by the length of the 'pyramid inch', produces the date of 4004 BC, the date advocated for the foundation of the world by James Ussher, Archbishop of Armagh, in Latin in 1650 and in English in 1658. Actually he put it specifically on the late evening of 22 October 4004 BC. For many years this date appeared printed as a marginal note in copies of the Authorised Bible. A second example relates to the pyramid's prophetical function: if measurements are taken from the entrance through the corridors, up through the Grand Gallery and to a point in the entrance passage to the King's Chamber where a mark is apparent on the granite wall, and again subject to division by the 'pyramid inch', the resulting answer given is 1914 – the year of the outbreak of the First World War, in many people's minds the Armageddon, the last battle, of the Bible. Smyth's work attracted many followers, and still does; amongst the most recent publications based on it is Peter Tomkins's *Secrets of the Great Pyramid* (1971). Egyptologists tend to regard followers of the 'pyramid inch' theories as 'pyramid cranks'.

Curiously, it was because of Piazzi Smyth's theories that the first proper detailed survey of the Great Pyramid was undertaken. Flinders Petrie's father, William Petrie, was most interested in Smyth's suggestions and resolved that he and his son would travel to Egypt and together survey the Great Pyramid with the greatest possible accuracy to prove the veracity of Smyth's theories. In the event, the older Petrie was unable to make the journey and it was left to the young William Matthew Flinders Petrie to go, complete with surveying gear, much of which was home-made since he and his father had a great interest in mathematics and had previously surveyed and charted a number of British prehistoric monuments. Petrie arrived in Egypt in December 1880 and commenced work. A strange, tall figure striding about with his surveying equipment, he presented quite a spectacle, even more so when he found it difficult to work in the heat of the internal passages and so resorted to wearing only pink longjohns.

Petrie's publication of *The Pyramids and Temples of Giza* in 1883, far from proving Piazzi Smyth right, completely refuted his arguments by providing accurate measurements that totally belied the so-called credibility of Smyth's calculations. Despite the somewhat primitive surveying equipment that he used, Petrie's measurements have withstood the test of time remarkably well. Even when more modern instruments were used in the government survey in 1925 by J.H. Cole, only occasional variations were noted.

Interest in the pyramids of Giza never flags. In the 1960s a team from Berkeley University, California, installed very sensitive computer-linked equipment in the burial chamber of the Second Pyramid to measure certain rays passing through the bulk of the pyramid and, by computer scan of the results registered, ascertain if there might be any hitherto undiscovered chambers. The result was negative. In September 1986 a French team was given permission by the Egyptian Antiquities Organisation to use high-velocity drills at certain points in the corridors of the Great Pyramid to drill deep behind the blocks to see if there were any concealed chambers. At the time of writing nothing has been found.

The Great Pyramid still has one secret, but it is outside it, not inside. In May 1954 a young Egyptian archaeologist, Kamal al-Mallakh, was given the task of clearing the debris from the south side of the pyramid. He found there a series of 41 large blocks of Tura limestone, securely fitted together. They covered a pit about 30 m (97 ft) long cut into the bed-rock. The pit had a revetted edge so that the sealing blocks had made it completely airtight (Figure 17). Within the pit, partly dismantled because it was 10 metres too long for the pit, was found a complete ancient

17 *Photograph (taken in 1963) from the top of the Great Pyramid down the south side showing the shed housing the Cheops boat. Just beyond it and to the right is the open pit with revetted edges in which the boat was found. This is now incorporated in the new Boat Museum on the site*

Egyptian wooden boat, perfectly preserved and composed of 1,274 pieces of wood with not a single metal nail in it. Boat pits are known associated with several of the pyramids – there are three such examples open close to the Great Pyramid – but all had been robbed in antiquity or their wooden contents destroyed by time. The boats were an important part of the funerary ritual and provision for the dead pharaoh in the next world. They are variously referred to as either funerary boats or solar boats – it being thought that at least two of those provided would serve the pharaoh as he journeyed through the daytime with the sun-god in the hereafter and as he progressed through the twelve hours of the night under the earth.

The evidence is that Cheops' boat (for it was his, and graffiti on the sealing blocks indicated that the burial had been completed by his son and successor Redjedef), did sail at least once on water. Perhaps it had been used to carry Cheops' embalmed body on its last journey across the Nile to the foot of the Causeway leading up to the Giza plateau. After many years of careful research, principally by Haj Ahmed Youssef, the carefully restored and reconstructed boat was placed on public exhibition in March 1982 in a specifically designed boat-shaped museum. It not only displays the boat in a magnificent way but also incorporates the original deep pit in which it was found.

The Great Pyramid's still undiscovered secret? Immediately behind and beyond the pit where the first boat was found is another series of sealing blocks over another pit. There is every reason to believe that a similar boat lies buried there. Whilst the first boat had a cabin amidships and oars, in all probability the second boat will be provided with a sail. Wooden models of ships found in Middle Kingdom tombs, as well as those shown on Old Kingdom reliefs, show two kinds of boat – one to be rowed downstream with the north-flowing current, the other with a sail set to propel it south against the current, helped by the prevailing north wind.

The Great Pyramid is truly one of the Seven Wonders of the Ancient World – it is the oldest of them, the only largely surviving one, and it has always had a stirring effect on the mind of humanity. The Arab proverb well sums up its impact: 'Man fears Time, yet Time fears the pyramids.'

THE HANGING GARDENS
OF BABYLON

IRVING L. FINKEL

IT MUST be admitted at the outset that the Hanging Gardens of Babylon, although famed far and wide as one of the celebrated Seven Wonders of the World, have never been conclusively identified nor, indeed, has their existence been proved (Figure 18). Our evidence for the gardens is late, 'classical allusions merely, drawn from the pagan authors' to paraphrase Dr Chasuble, so the intention of the present chapter is to look briefly at the background of the city of Babylon itself, to investigate what the later authors wrote about the gardens, to look at other royal gardens, and to compare the classical information with the results of the archaeological investigation of that venerable city.

Babylon was the capital city of the land of Babylonia, situated on the river Euphrates, some 400 miles north-west of the Persian Gulf, and over 600 miles east of the Mediterranean in what is now Iraq. The city first came to prominence in the ancient world under its famous king Hammurabi (1792–1750 BC), who produced the Code of Laws forever associated with his name which is now housed in the Louvre Museum, Paris. The fortunes of the city fluctuated in the centuries following his reign but reached their peak under the rulers of the Neo-Babylonian or Chaldaean dynasty. This period saw a series of impressive and memorable rulers whose names have survived the disappearance of Mesopotamian civilisation. The founder of the dynasty, Nabopolassar (625–605 BC), was responsible with his allies, the Medes and the Scythians, for the final downfall in 612 BC of Assyria, whose might had dominated politics and private lives alike for generations. His son Nebuchadnezzar II (604–562 BC), known to the Book of Daniel as Nebuchadrezzar, was one of

Mesopotamia's most illustrious and effective kings. He pursued an active policy of extending and securing his empire, fighting campaigns in Syria, Palestine and Egypt, which, as chronicled in the Bible, led to the removal of Jehoiakin, King of Judah, and many prisoners to Babylon in 597 BC (II Kings 24: 14–16), and later to the destruction of the Temple in Jerusalem and the wholesale removal of the Jews to Babylon in 586 BC. The last king of the dynasty was Nabonidus (555–539 BC).

At home Nebuchadnezzar was an indefatigable builder. A vast labour force was put to work producing mud bricks in uncountable numbers which, under the supervision of the royal architects, became palaces, temples, gates and magnificent city walls, on a scale that must have overawed visiting dignitaries and subject peoples alike. A particular hallmark of this architecture was the use of blue glazed bricks to face the most imposing monuments, while similar bricks with moulded reliefs of lions, bulls and dragons (Figure 19) were added to reinforce the splendour and power of the king's city. Herodotus' classic description of Babylon reflects the city of Nebuchadnezzar's

18 *Fischer von Erlach's imaginative eighteenth-century engraving of Babylon with the Hanging Gardens in the background*

19 *A dragon represented in relief in glazed bricks on the Ishtar Gateway, as reconstructed in the Staatliche Museum, East Berlin*

making and such monuments as survive to this day are largely his work.

Thanks principally to the excavations carried out by the German archaeologist Robert Koldewey at the beginning of this century a great deal of the city has been uncovered. In addition to the remains themselves, the historian of Babylon has contemporary written cuneiform evidence from the kings themselves, who, with a burning desire to keep their achievements in the minds of the gods, and with more than an eye to posterity, recorded lengthy descriptions of their building programmes, their restorations and innovations (Figure 20).

Such building inscriptions are characteristic of the dynasty and the sorting out of the often broken sources and the reconstruction of the cuneiform texts is a still-continuing work for modern scholars. In addition to the kings' own narratives, a further boon is a composition known as the Topography of Babylon, five tablets in length, which purports to describe the city in full, naming its streets and shrines, gates and temples, an invaluable sourcebook for those interested in Babylon in the first millennium BC.

20 *Cylinder inscribed with Babylonian cuneiform. It describes work on the temples, walls and ziggurats of Babylon and Borsippa by Nebuchadnezzar, developing the work of his father. (British Museum)*

In our pursuit of the Hanging Gardens, then, we must pause to reflect on the unexpected silence on the part of all these native cuneiform texts on the question of anything that could be identified with the fabled Wonder. No Babylonian inscription refers to a building that can plausibly be identified with a royal and spectacular garden, especially one that, if the later accounts shortly to be quoted are to be believed, was such an extraordinary technological innovation. Let us then look at what may be gleaned from the later writers on the subject of the Hanging Gardens of Babylon.

There are five principal writers who have left us a description to lend some substance to our idea of the gardens. The authority whose testimony on Babylonian matters must be accorded the most sympathetic reception is undoubtedly Berossus. Berossus was a contemporary of Alexander the Great; his birth is usually placed somewhere after 350 BC. He tells us that he was a priest of Bel (that is Marduk, the national god of Babylonia), of Chaldaean origin. Later in life he left Babylon and went to live on the island of Cos, but about 280 BC he produced a remarkable book called the *Babyloniaca*, one of a pair (the other was concerned with Assyria), which he wrote in order to explain the culture of Mesopotamia to the Greeks, to whom the cuneiform world was a closed book. From what survives of Berossus' work, he was evidently familiar at first hand with the traditional cuneiform literature in Sumerian and Akkadian that had been handed down

*21 School tablet from Babylon
containing the beginning of the*
Topography of Babylon *in Greek
script; the other side contained the
same text in cuneiform. Perhaps* c.
300 BC. (British Museum)

literally over millennia, and that was still current in the academies
of Babylon (Figure 21). The *Babyloniaca* was dedicated by its
author to Antiochus I (281–260 BC), who is known to have been
favourably disposed towards the temple and priests of Marduk
and Babylonian learning generally. The Greeks tended to see
other peoples as barbarians and the book was probably not widely
read; it does not itself survive. We are fortunate, however, that
later writers have quoted from it and thus preserved much of that
invaluable book. What does survive overlaps to a large extent
with Mesopotamian ideas and traditions known from cuneiform
texts. Among his notes Berossus ascribes the Hanging Gardens of
Babylon to Nabouchodonosorous (Nebuchadnezzar II). The
passage is twice quoted for us by Josephus, the later writer who
attempted to describe the history and culture of the Jews in much
the same spirit as led Berossus to take up his pen. These are his
descriptions of Nebuchadnezzar's achievement:

> At his palace he had knolls made of stone which he shaped
> like mountains and planted with all kinds of trees. Further-
> more, he had a so-called pensile paradise planted because his
> wife, who came from Media, longed for such, which was the
> custom in her homeland. (*Jewish Antiquities* X, 11)
>
> . . . and, within this palace he erected lofty stone terraces, in
> which he closely reproduced mountain scenery, completing

the resemblence by planting them with all manner of trees and constructing the so-called Hanging Garden; because his wife, having been brought up in Media, had a passion for mountain surroundings. (*Contra Apionem* I, 19)

Native sources are silent on the question of this wife of Nebuchadnezzar, but a dynastic marriage between the Babylonians and the Medes is historically very plausible and we are informed by Berossus that this Median princess was called Amytis.

The four other descriptions of the gardens to be quoted contain more precise technological details. Next to be cited is the description by Diodorus Siculus, who lived around the middle of the first century BC:

There was also, beside the acropolis, the Hanging Garden, as it is called, which was built, not by Semiramis, but by a later Syrian king to please one of his concubines; for she, they say, being a Persian by race and longing for the meadows of her mountains, asked the king to imitate, through the artifice of a planted garden, the distinctive landscape of Persia. The park extended four plethra on each side, and since the approach to the garden sloped like a hillside and the several parts of the structure rose from one another tier on tier, the appearance of the whole resembled that of a theatre. When the ascending terraces had been built, there had been constructed beneath them galleries which carried the entire weight of the planted garden and rose little by little one above the other along the approach; and the uppermost gallery, which was fifty cubits high, bore the highest surface of the park, which was made level with the circuit wall of the battlements of the city. Furthermore, the walls, which had been constructed at great expense, were twenty-two feet thick, while the passageway between each two walls was ten feet wide. The roofs of the galleries were covered over with beams of stone sixteen foot long, inclusive of the overlap, and four feet wide. The roof above these beams had first a layer of reeds laid in great quantities of bitumen, over this two courses of baked brick bonded by cement, and as a third layer a covering of lead, to the end that the moisture from the soil might not penetrate beneath. On all this again the earth had been piled to a depth sufficient for the roots of the largest trees; and the ground, when levelled off, was thickly planted with trees of every kind that, by their great size or any other charm, could give pleasure to the beholder. And since the galleries, each projecting beyond another, all received the light, they contained many royal lodges of every description; and there was one gallery which contained openings leading from the topmost surface and machines for supplying the gardens with water, the machines raising the water in great abundance from the river, although no one outside could see it being done. (Diodorus Siculus II, 10)

Scholars have concluded that this description of Diodorus derives in part from a lost History of Alexander written by one Cleitarchus of Alexandria in the last years of the fourth century BC. Cleitarchus was born at the time of Alexander's defeat of the Persians under Darius III. It is likely that even if he never visited Babylon himself he would have had the opportunity to talk to soldiers who had served under Alexander and seen the city for themselves. Further information comes from one Ctesias, a Greek physician who, as a prisoner of war, worked as a doctor at the Persian court around 400 BC. The same sources probably lie behind the next report, that of Quintus Curtius Rufus from his own *History of Alexander* (V. 1. 35):

On the summit of the citadel are the Hanging Gardens, a trite theme with the Greek poets; they equal in height the walls of the town, and their numerous lofty trees afford a grateful shade. The trees are twelve feet in circumference, and fifty feet in height: nor, in their native soil, could they be more productive. Supporting these, are twenty dense walls, distant from each other twenty feet, surmounted with ranges of stone piers, over which is extended a quadrangular pavement of stone, strong enough to bear earth amassed high, and water supplied for irrigation. A distant spectator of these groves would suppose them to be woods nodding on their mountains. Notwithstanding time destroys, by insensible corrosion, not only human works, but even nature herself; yet this pile, pressed with the roots, and loaded with the trunks of so gigantic a plantation, still remains entire. Tradition affirms, that a king of Assyria, reigning in Babylon, executed this work to gratify his queen, who, delighting in forest scenery, persuaded her husband to imitate the beauties of nature by a garden on this imperial scale.

Strabo says on the subject, drawing it is believed on a lost text by Onesicritus, who also wrote during the reign of Alexander the Great:

Babylon, too, lies in a plain; and the circuit of its wall is three hundred and eighty-five stadia. The thickness of its wall is thirty-two feet; the height thereof between the towers is fifty cubits; that of the towers is sixty cubits; and the passage on top of the wall is such that four-horse chariots can easily pass one another; and it is on this account that this and the hanging garden are called one of the Seven Wonders of the World. The garden is quadrangular in shape, and each side is four plethra in length. It consists of arched vaults, which are situated, one after another, on checkered, cube-like foundations. The checkered foundations, which are hollowed out, are covered so deep with earth that they admit of the largest of trees, having been constructed of baked brick and asphalt – the foundations themselves and the vaults and the arches. The ascent to the uppermost terrace-roofs is made by a stairway; and alongside these stairs there were screws, through which the water was continually conducted up into the garden from the Euphrates by those appointed for this purpose, for the river, a stadium in width, flows through the middle of the city; and the garden is on the bank of the river. (*Geography*, XVI, 1.5)

Finally, we may give a voice to Philo of Byzantium, who probably flourished around 250 BC, and whose list of the Seven Wonders of the World is the one that has gained most currency in tradition. He says about Babylon's celebrated garden:

The Hanging Garden [is so-called because it] has plants cultivated at a height above ground level, and the roots of the trees are embedded in an upper terrace rather than in the earth. This is the technique of its construction. The whole mass is supported on stone columns, so that the entire underlying space is occupied by carved column bases. The columns carry beams set at very narrow intervals. The beams are palm trunks, for this type of wood – unlike all others – does not rot and, when it is damp and subjected to heavy pressure, it curves upwards. Moreover it does itself give nourishment to the root branches and fibres, since it admits extraneous matter into its folds and crevices. This structure supports an extensive and deep mass of earth, in which are planted broad-leaved trees of the sort that are commonly found in gardens, a wide variety of flowers of all species and, in brief, everything that is most agreeable to the eye and conducive to the enjoyment of pleasure. The whole area is ploughed in the same way as solid ground, and is just as suitable as other soil for grafting and propagation. Thus it happens that a ploughed field lies above the heads of those who walk between the columns below. Yet while the upper surface of the earth is trampled underfoot, the lower and denser soil closest to the supporting framework remains undisturbed and virgin. Streams of water emerging from elevated sources flow partly in a straight line down sloping channels, and are partly forced upwards through bends and spirals to gush out higher up, being impelled through the twists of these devices by mechanical forces. So, brought together in frequent and plentiful outlets at a high level, these waters irrigate the whole garden, saturating the deep roots of the plants and keeping the whole area of cultivation continually moist. Hence the grass is permanently green, and the leaves of trees grow firmly attached to supple branches, and increasing in size and succulence with the constant humidity. For the root [system] is kept saturated and sucks up the all-pervading supply of water, wandering in interlaced channels beneath the ground, and securely maintaining the well-established and excellent quality of the trees. This is a work of art of royal luxury [lit. 'riotous living'], and its most striking feature is that the labour of cultivation is suspended above the heads of the spectators. (Translated by Professor David Oates)

It says something about Philo the great engineer that, if he really lived about 250 BC he did not even have a good second-hand account of the Hanging Gardens. After all, the palace of Nebuchadnezzar was sufficiently well preserved in 323 for Alexander to die there.

This, then, is principally what is bequeathed us by the pagan authors as the received knowledge about the Hanging Gardens. If any credence is to be given to their joint accounts, the archaeological evidence speaks in favour of Berossus' statement that it was King Nebuchadnezzar who was responsible. Before investigating the city of Babylon itself, a word should be said about other royal gardens from ancient Mesopotamia, since there is plentiful evidence that earlier kings prized their gardens, and devoted much attention to them.

Sennacherib (704–681 BC), the 'Assyrian who came down like a wolf on the fold' in Byron's words, is known to have been personally interested in botany. He had laid out an extensive garden near his palace at Nineveh and went out of his way to have it stocked with rare and exotic plants, herbs and trees collected in some cases from far-flung places. It appears, indeed, that cotton was even imported from India, if that is the correct interpretation of the quaint phrase 'trees which produce wool' which is used in his description. Sennacherib went to great trouble to supply Nineveh with reliable water supplies, damming the River Khosr, probably to guard against the possibility of siege. He even had built several miles of aqueduct replacing earlier work, of which extensive traces survive. One can thus be sure that elaborate provisions were taken to ensure adequate irrigation for his gardens.

Other earlier Assyrian kings have left us accounts of their gardens in their royal inscriptions. Earlier at Nineveh Tiglath-Pileser I (1115–1077 BC) prided himself on opulent gardens and orchards, while at another Assyrian capital, Nimrud (Biblical Calah), Assurnasirpal II (883–859 BC), has left us a long inscription on a stone stela describing how he planted royal gardens near the citadel and the river Tigris which were also stocked with a range of species from foreign parts that had become available as a result of energetic military campaigns:

> canal-water came flowing down from above through the gardens; the paths are full of scent; the waterfalls [sparkle] like the stars of heaven in the garden of pleasure. The pomegranate trees, which are clothed with clusters of fruit like vines, enrich the breezes in this garden of delight. I, Assur-nāsir-apli, gather fruit continuously in the garden of joys like a squirrel(?). (Assurnasirpal stela)

A complete cuneiform tablet now in the British Museum is a later copy prepared from an earlier manuscript that lists varieties of plants found in the garden of the Babylonian king Marduk-apla-iddina (721–710 and 703 BC), the Biblical Merodach-Baladan (Figure 22). Sixty-seven varieties are listed, mostly vegetables. A famous relief of the last great king of Assyria, Assurbanipal (668–627 BC), also in the British Museum, shows us part of the royal gardens in his capital at Nineveh (Figure 23).

Given, then, the attention paid by the later writers to the Hanging Gardens, and the well-documented tradition of royal gardens in Mesopotamia, we may suspend our scepticism for the moment. Assuming that something extraordinary of the kind was to be seen in Babylon in its heyday, let us look at the city itself to

22 *Cuneiform tablet from Babylon listing plants in the garden of Marduk-apla-iddina. It dates from the seventh century BC but is a copy of an older text. (British Museum)*

see where they might have been located.

Babylon is the largest city of ancient Mesopotamia, exceeding even Nineveh, covering an area of some 850 hectares, as can be seen in a schematic plan of the inner city at the time of Nebuchadnezzar (Figure 24). The city itself was surrounded by double fortification walls founded by Nabopolassar and completed by Nebuchadnezzar. These walls must have presented an overpowering spectacle even from a long way off, and we have noticed above that for Strabo at least these walls effectively constituted one of the Seven Wonders of the World in their own right. Towering over the city was the ziggurat, located in the vast temple complex dedicated to Marduk, near his temple Esagila. We know something of Babylon in the century after Nebuchadnezzar from the *Histories* of Herodotus. Herodotus, born between 490 and 480 BC, often styled the 'Father of History', is assuredly the best known Greek writer. His famous work, which documents the fatal struggle between the Greeks and the Persians, contains a wealth of information about the ancient world, including many fascinating details about Egypt and Babylon. This is how he describes Marduk's temple buildings:

23 *Assyrian wall relief from the palace of Assurbanipal showing part of a royal garden. (British Museum)*

There is a fortress in the middle of each half of the city: in one the royal palace surrounded by a wall of great strength, in the other the temple of Bel, the Babylonian Zeus. The temple is a square building, two furlongs each way, with bronze gates, and was still in existence in my time; it has a solid central tower, one furlong square, with a second erected on top of it and then a third, and so on up to eight. All eight towers can be climbed by a spiral way running round the outside, and about half way up there are seats for those who make the ascent to rest on. On the summit of the topmost tower stands a great temple with a fine large couch on it, richly covered, and a golden table beside it. The shrine contains no image and no one spends the night there except (if we may believe the Chaldeans who are the priests of Bel) one Assyrian woman, all alone, whoever it may be that the god has chosen. The Chaldeans also say – though I do not believe them – that the god enters the temple in person and takes his rest upon the bed. There is a similar story told by the Egyptians at Thebes, where a woman always passes the

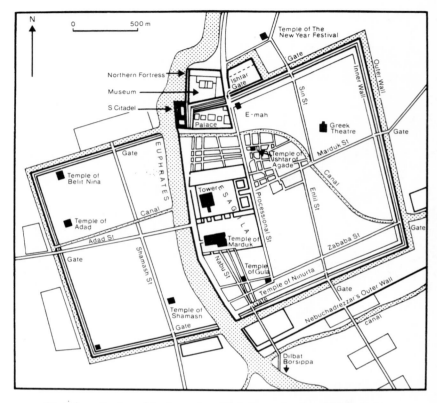

24 *Schematic plan of the inner city of Babylon at the time of Nebuchadnezzar II. (After J. Oates)*

night in the temple of the Theban Zeus and is forbidden, so they say, like the woman in the temple at Babylon, to have any intercourse with men; and there is yet another instance in the Lycian town of Patara, where the priestess who delivers the oracles when required (for there is not always an oracle there) is shut up in the temple during the night.

In the temple of Babylon there is a second shrine lower down, in which is a great sitting figure of Bel, all of gold on a golden throne, with a golden table standing beside it. I was told by the Chaldeans that, to make all this, more than twenty-two tons of gold were used.

The ziggurrat, of course, strikes the keynote of Mesopotamian civilisation. As reported by Herodotus the ziggurrat takes the form of a stepped tower of mud bricks surmounted by a small shrine. Ziggurrats survive to a greater or lesser extent in many of the ancient cities of Iraq, but that of Babylon is the best known. In historical tradition it is often identified with the Tower of Babel in the Book of Genesis, and in the last century there was a flurry of debate as to whether the Tower of Babel was that of Babylon, nearby Borsippa, or Aqar Quf. Of the authorities quoted here Herodotus is the nearest in time to the period of Nebuchadnezzar and it is a surprising fact that he makes no mention of the Hanging Gardens in his narrative. This indeed is a difficult objection to answer. Some have thought that the gardens may have been placed on the ziggurrat itself. This would accord with our other accounts in one respect, namely that the function of the ziggurrat (in the broadest terms) was to bring man as near as possible to the gods; the stepped form that they always took could have led to the story of a man-made imitation of a mountain on a grand scale. This is, of course, a valid point but it overlooks the insurmountable difficulties of irrigation, and it can be ruled out that the ziggurrat at Babylon was ever covered with greenery. For those who would discount the Hanging Gardens as the stuff of myth, however, the ziggurrat can be seen as the solid reality behind the work of poets.

The inner city of Babylon was characterised by a blend of magnificence and order. The streets are laid out parallel to the river and at right angles to one another, in a curiously modern-looking way. Eight gates provided access to the city, of which the most familiar is that usually called the Ishtar Gate. This was situated roughly in the middle of the northern walls and gave on to the equally famous Processional Way. A reconstruction of this magnificent architecture, as assembled by the archaeologists, is to be seen in the Vorderasiatisches Museum in East Berlin (Figure 25). Here in particular liberal use was made of the blue-glazed bricks referred to above (see Figure 19) and it was through this gate that successive kings, Nebuchadnezzar, Darius and Alexander, rode into the city with fanfares, entourage and splendour.

At the time of Nebuchadnezzar there were several palaces in Babylon. The Northern Palace is situated just beyond the city walls, while relatively little remains of the so-called Summer Palace. The most important was the Southern Palace, which contained five large courtyards surrounded by a maze of chambers and apartments. Here was located the royal throne room, the

25 *The Ishtar Gateway from Babylon, as reconstructed in the Staatliche Museum, East Berlin*

scene of Belshazzar's Feast as described in the Bible, and the place where Alexander the Great died while still mourning Hephaestion. The same glazed bricks were put to use to ornament this palace. Later in his reign Nebuchadnezzar built a second palace to the north of this principal residence where, among other things, archaeologists uncovered what must have been a museum: inscriptions dating back as early as the end of the third millennium BC had been carefully collected and hoarded. Such an antiquarian interest seems to have characterised more than one king of the Neo-Babylonian dynasty.

It was while excavating the north-east corner of the Southern Palace that Koldewey came upon the building known as the Vaulted Building that he tentatively identified with the Hanging Gardens of Babylon. This took the form of a subterranean crypt consisting of a series of fourteen vaulted rooms, as Koldewey described it:

> Fourteen cells, similar in size and shape, balance each other on the two sides of a central passage, and are surrounded by a strong wall. Round this slightly irregular quadrangle runs a

narrow corridor, of which the far side to the north and east is in large measure formed of the outer wall of the Citadel, while other ranges of similar cells abut on it to the west and south. In one of these western cells is a well which differs from all other wells known either in Babylon or elsewhere in the ancient world. It has three shafts placed close to each other, a square one in the centre and oblong ones on each side, an arrangement for which I can see no other explanation than that a mechanical hydraulic machine stood here, which worked on the same principle as our chain pump, where buckets attached to a chain work on a wheel placed over the wall. A whim works the wheel in endless rotation. This contrivance, which is used today in this neighbourhood, and is called a *dolab* (water bucket), would provide a continuous flow of water.

And, later,

Further observation of the ground-plan shows that the central chambers with the same span as the outside row have thicker walls. The only explanation for this must be that the former were more heavily weighted than the latter, a supposition which is corroborated by the expansion joints that surround them, by which the vaulting itself is disconnected from the wall surrounding it on all four sides. Owing to this the whole of the 14 barrel-vaultings could move as freely upwards or downwards within the enclosing quadrangle as the joint of a telescope. In this respect the vaulted building is unique among the buildings of Babylon, and in another respect also it is exceptional. Stone was used in the building, as is proved by the numerous fragments, shapeless as they now are, that are found in the ruins. In excavating this makes a far deeper impression than the mere report can do.

There are only two places where hewn stone appears in any large quantity – in the Vaulted Building and on the north wall of the Kasr, and it is remarkable that in all the literature referring to Babylon, including the cuneiform inscriptions, stone is only mentioned as used in two places, in the north wall of the Kasr and in the hanging gardens.

Having proposed the identification of this building with the site of the Gardens Koldewey remarks: 'That the identification when studied in detail bristles with difficulties will surprise no one who has more than once had to bring ancient statements of facts into accordance with discoveries of the present day.'

When he first made this suggestion Koldewey made no claim to certainty; the idea was merely advanced for consideration. However, in later publications the identity was felt to be more secure and many subsequent popular writers have taken the mere suggestion to be fact. Discussion of the Seven Wonders of the World tends to make the identification without question and visitors to the site itself nowadays are shown what remains of the building and told that this is what survives of Nebuchadnezzar's famous construction. Recently the crumbling brickwork has been restored by the Directorate-General of Antiquities, Baghdad, following another investigation of the Vaulted Building.

A result of these excavations were some refinements of Koldewey's measurements and other details were added, but nothing new emerged that helps identify the original use of the building.

We may thus summarise the points raised by Koldewey in favour of his identification as follows:

(a) Use of worked stone, scarcely used elsewhere.
(b) Unusually thick walls apparently designed to take a heavy superstructure.
(c) Presence of a well of unparalleled type.

Having assembled all the information he could, Koldewey then produced a reconstruction drawing of the Hanging Gardens of Babylon as he conceived them (Figure 26).

For many years after the appearance of the final reports on the excavations by the German team most scholars let the subject lie, presumably since the lack of new evidence has meant that little more could be said. Recently, however, several scholars have returned to the problems of the Hanging Gardens afresh, notably Dr W. Nagel and Professor D.J. Wiseman, upon whose work many of the present observations are based. Several cogent arguments against Koldewey's identification have been raised.

In general terms the complex of arched rooms in the Vaulted Building has been shown to have had other, more prosaic uses. They are now considered more likely to have been storerooms, since an archive of cuneiform tablets was found there, dating from the tenth to the thirty-fifth year of Nebuchadnezzar. These texts are lists of rations, in oil and barley, that were to be disbursed to groups of foreign exiles held captive in Babylon at the time. Extraordinarily enough Jehoiakin of Judah is actually mentioned by name in some of these tablets together with his entourage, a remarkable instance of cuneiform sources tying in neatly with the Biblical narrative. Other groups of captives are also mentioned and thus it has been suggested that the strength implicit in the architecture might suggest that an element of security lay behind the design. It has, moreover, been doubted that the strength of these walls was really adequate to support a garden, but rather that it served to support a continuation of the Procession Street.

Another crucial difficulty is the distance of the Vaulted Building from water supplies and the river. Note here especially Strabo's clear statement that the gardens were situated by the river. Another consideration is how this location works in view of the design of the Southern Palace as a whole. Anyone who wished to enter the gardens coming from Nebuchadnezzar's Palace would have had to cross over the administrative courts and apartments, since this would sacrifice the privacy no doubt required by the king and his family, not to say harem. As a result, scholars have looked elsewhere in the city for a suitable location.

26 *Koldewey's reconstruction of the Vaulted Building as the Hanging Gardens. (After Koldewey)*

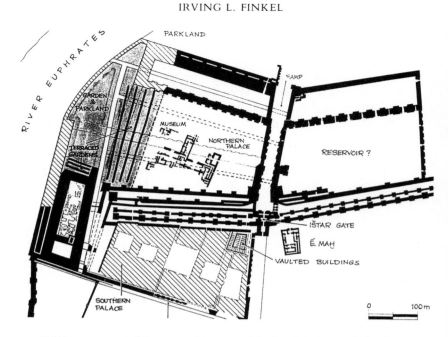

27 *Reconstruction of the proposed location of the Royal ('Hanging') Gardens at Babylon. (After Wiseman)*

The reader's attention is directed to the second map of the northern city (Figure 27). Comparison with the larger scale map in Figure 24 will help to place the principal features. Koldewey's Vaulted Building is situated approximately in the middle. Wiseman has proposed that the Hanging Gardens be placed 'on, and to the north of, the massive (110 × 230m) "Western Outwork" building between the Western Palace, known to have been occupied by Nebuchadnezzar and his queen, and the R. Euphrates.' He continues:

> Excavations on the 'Western Outwork' revealed the lower levels of a small, palace-like building which could have been a 'summer-house, pavilion or kiosk' . . . but without any entrance which must therefore have been at an upper level by raised way or bridge direct from the palace platform.
> That these gardens were confined to terraces on the East bank of the Euphrates is unlikely in that they would have been exposed to the westerly desert winds and have had no privacy. It is probable that they were continued on terraces to

28 *Artist's reconstruction panoramic view of the Royal ('Hanging') Gardens of Babylon. (Courtesy of Professor D.J. Wiseman)*

the north protected by walls, and formed an amphitheatre-like layout visible from the palace itself. This would have had the advantage of ready access also to extended gardens which may have reached as far as the bît akîti temple and gardens which lay to the north outside the citadel. Nebuchadnezzar claims to have built a structure on superimposed terraces when extending his palace across the double defence walls of the original 'Southern Citadel' to what is sometimes designated the Northern Palace. Here were found deep drains suitable also for extensive irrigation. They connected with the Östliche Ausfallvorwerk which Bergamini has suggested to be a reservoir to ensure the movement of water throughout the extra-mural moat system rather than a bastion.

The Iraqi scholar Dr Mu'ayyad Damerji has pointed out that the two massive walls by the river (some 25m thick) may have been stepped and covered with bitumen and matting to form terraces. In his description of the construction Nebuchadnezzar describes the building as being made 'like a great fortification wall' which could conceivably reflect an imitation of a mountain scene.

Proceeding from his studies Professor Wiseman has recently produced a reconstructed panorama of the Royal Gardens of Nebuchadnezzar in this new location, which attempts to marry the traditional accounts with a study of the archaeological possibilities of the site (Figure 28); it surely represents the most that can be done with the present evidence.

Sherlock Holmes once surprised Dr Watson by deducing that a man was decidedly intelligent on the basis of a hat which he had left behind, because his large cranium bespoke an ample brain, and 'a man with so large a brain must have something in it'. A similar argument might be applied to the question of the Hanging Gardens. Even allowing for an over-credulous interest in travellers' accounts and for the repetition from book to book of information not personally tested by each writer, the testimony of the classical writers on the Hanging Gardens is impressive and cannot just lightly be dismissed. As we have seen, the attribution of the work to Nebuchadnezzar by Berossus would make sense with what we know of his building activities, and we know that a royal garden was traditionally considered to be an appropriate feature of a Mesopotamian palace. The absence of references to it in cuneiform texts is admittedly a difficulty, graver perhaps than its omission in Herodotus' description of Babylon. New discoveries in Assyriology are, however, being made all the time and it is always possible that the excavations at Babylon currently being conducted by the Iraqi State Organization for Antiquities and Heritage will one day uncover a text that will throw direct light on the matter. So, while the question can at present only really be left open, the possibility is there that the Hanging Gardens were once to be seen silhouetted against the darkening sky over Babylon. Even if, after all, the gardens as described to us never existed, the city walls did and still do in part and, according to Strabo's view, Babylon itself must in any case qualify for inclusion among the Seven Wonders of the World.

THE STATUE OF ZEUS
AT OLYMPIA

MARTIN J. PRICE

THE WHOLE world knows of the Olympic games, but not many realise that the statue of the god in whose honour the games were held in ancient times was also one of the Seven Wonders of the World. Olympia was a place of worship. The temple and altar of Zeus, the king of the gods, drew pilgrims from all parts of the Greek world and one important element of the ritual practised there was the celebration of athletic contests. The games were revived in 1896 and victory in this arena is viewed by many to be almost equal to victory in the world of politics. So it was in ancient Greece. Athletes gathered at Olympia for these games from every quarter of the known world and this remote spot in the western part of southern Greece became the focal point of the world's attention.

The participants had to be of Greek blood, for the origin of the games lay in religious ritual. 'Barbarians', non-Greeks, could not worship in the sanctuary of Zeus and could not take part in the games. Heralds travelled to the furthest outposts of Greek civilisation to invite the Greeks to take part. From Sicily and Cyrene, from Syria and Egypt, from Macedonia and Asia, they flocked to Olympia and, while the games were in progress, it was an honoured tradition that war should cease between Greek states.

The southern land-mass of Greece is known as the Peloponnese – the isle of Pelops – and it is this Pelops who was connected with the institution of the Olympic games. A small kingdom in the west of the Peloponnese named Pisa was ruled, it was said, by King Oenomaus. In his territory lay Olympia, a fertile area made sacred to Zeus, the king of the gods, and to Mother Earth. Countless worshippers used to go there to seek divine help for their own harvest. King Oenomaus was warned by a prophecy that he would be killed by his son-in-law, so he watched with worried anticipation as his daughter Hippodameia came of age. He insisted that every suitor for her hand should take part in a chariot race with him from Olympia to the temple of the sea-god, Poseidon, at Isthmia near Corinth, some eighty miles to the north-east. The suitor was given a fair start and it was agreed that, if he was victorious, he should win Hippodameia and the throne of Pisa, but if the king caught up with him he should die. Thirteen suitors accepted the challenge and thirteen died. Finally young Pelops came forward. Some say that the god Poseidon intervened and caused Oenomaus' chariot to crash. Others say that Pelops bribed the groom to remove the axle pin and replace it with a pin of wax. Whatever the cause, Oenomaus crashed and was killed. Pelops married Hippodameia and succeeded to the throne.

The chariot race instituted at Olympia with other events was believed by many Greeks to commemorate the victory that led to Pelops' accession. Others believed that in fact Herakles, son of Zeus and the hero of all who would lay claim to strength and stamina, had founded the games at Olympia in honour of his father. Today we know that athletic games were often connected with funerary arrangements. Like an Irish wake they dissipated the grief of those who mourned. Here at Olympia the games probably began as a commemorative festival held by the Greeks of the area around the tomb of Pelops, who had so won the favour of the gods. His tomb or, rather, cenotaph, was at the very heart of the sacred building complex. In time the emphasis changed. The games were celebrated more and more in honour of Zeus and the part of Pelops was less evident.

The Greeks had a very personal view of their gods. The direct action of the gods in human affairs was commonplace. Their home, it was believed, was at the top of Mount Olympus in Thessaly, 175 miles to the north of Olympia. Zeus was their king and, as such, he combined the almighty power of the great god of nature with the weaknesses of a human king plus the attributes of the just and loving father. On the one hand, he was Zeus the thunderer who wielded the thunderbolt of lightning. On the other, his weakness for the opposite sex threw his queen, Hera, into passionate rages. Yet again, he was the god of hospitality to whom offerings would be made at banquets. Olympia, the very name of which echoes Mount Olympus, was Zeus' second home and this became, as a result of the games, the centre of his worship for over a thousand years.

Today the wooded grove of the sacred precinct of Zeus in the fertile valley of the river Alphaeus, where it meets the Kladeus, is the haunt of pilgrims of another age. Tourists flock to admire the remains of this great and holy place. It is natural that archaeologists should have turned their resources to rediscovering the past history of this sanctuary. Since 1829 teams from France and Germany have uncovered an elaborate concourse of religious monuments which intermingle with the buildings that provided the more functional requirements of the athletes who every four years gathered for the games. The gymnasium and the stadium nestle beside the temples and votive offerings set up in gratitude by victors and their sponsors in the sanctuary.

Olympia was not a town, an urban community, but a shrine around which clustered buildings that served the needs of the many pilgrims who came to worship and to take part in the games. It was a mixture between Mecca, the great religious centre, and Wembley, famous as the centre of sport. As with any place where there is continuous human activity, buildings of all periods reflecting the growth of the sanctuary are scattered over the site.

The Greeks believed that the games began in 776 BC and they used that date as the base from which to count the passing years, as today we use the birth of Christ. Yet archaeologists have now found that people worshipped at Olympia from a much earlier date. The earliest buildings were of wood and mud brick, but as civilisation developed and the older buildings decayed, they were replaced by grander monuments of stone. The most magnificent building of them all was the temple dedicated to Zeus himself.

The temple was a grand structure built between the years 466 and 456 BC at a time when new techniques and new visions heralded the classical age of Greece. The architect was Libon, from the neighbouring city of Elis, and he chose for the construction a curious local stone, a conglomerate of fossil shells, poor, perhaps for the refinements of architectural mouldings but a gloriously natural fabric in which to honour Zeus the god of nature. The style of the building was that popular in southern Greece at the time, similar in many respects to the more famous Parthenon at Athens. It was austere in the so-called Doric style, and not a little heavy, without the flamboyance of that other temple amongst the Seven Wonders, the temple of Artemis at Ephesos.

The temple was the shrine of the god, but it was not created to house a congregation. The sacrifice, the main object of congregational devotion, was performed at the great altar of Zeus outside the temple. On the middle day of the Olympic games a hundred oxen were slaughtered there and burned in offering to Zeus. The ashes, mixed with water from the Alpheus river, were piled on the altar in a huge compacted mound which grew to enormous proportions over the centuries. The temple building was required to protect the sacred cult image from the elements. The figure represented to his worshippers the presence of Zeus himself, in the inner sanctuary of his temple, in the holy of holies. As time passed, Olympia came to be visited more for its magnificence and for its antiquity than for its sanctity and, like many cathedrals today, the temple had something of the atmosphere of a museum.

For many years after its completion the new temple must have housed an ancient or revered cult object, a misshapen piece of stone or wood perhaps, removed from an earlier, smaller shrine. The current taste of the fifth century BC demanded a much more impressive image. The council of the sanctuary appears to have searched long for a sculptor who could create a statue of sufficient majesty to embody the ideal of the king of the gods. At last they chose for this tremendous task Pheidias, son of Charmides, a citizen of Athens.

Pheidias had already sculpted two mighty statues for the Acropolis of his home city, both destined to remain for centuries amongst the most magnificent products of the classical age of sculpture. The first, a gigantic figure of the goddess Athena, stood in the open air. It was nearly ten metres high and it was said that her golden helmet could be seen by sailors far out to sea. The second was the awesome cult image of Athena, worked in ivory and gold, for her new temple on the Acropolis, the Parthenon. Pheidias also designed, and may have worked upon, the architectural sculptures that decorated the exterior of the Parthenon. Most of these now reside in the British Museum and they provide the only surviving sculpture that gives us a clue to Pheidias' own personal style.

Superb though his sculpture was recognised to be, Pheidias himself was forced to leave Athens in disgrace in 438 or 437 BC on completion of his Athena for the Parthenon. He was indicted by Menon, a fellow worker on the statue, for embezzlement of some of the gold provided for the work. It seems that Pheidias was unable to provide accurate accounts of the weight of gold used in each part of the statue and he preferred voluntary exile to public humiliation. In fact the charge was certainly made for political motives. Pheidias was a friend of the statesman Perikles whose vision and personal influence with the citizens was responsible for the glorious rebuilding of Athens after its destruction by the Persians in 480 BC. Perikles was not without his political enemies who did not fail to take every opportunity to discredit him. The humiliation of his friend the sculptor Pheidias was such an occasion.

Despite the charge, Pheidias came to Olympia soon after this to begin work on his masterpiece. It is a measure of the faith that the council at Olympia had in him, and of his real innocence of the charge laid against him at Athens, that he was given the commission for the new figure of Zeus. At Athens Pheidias had developed a technique that allowed statues of gold and ivory to be built of enormous size. First a wooden framework was erected on the spot at which the statue was to stand, fitting exactly the overall shape of the finished sculpture. Thin plates of ivory were carved to fit the flesh areas and sheets of precious metals were moulded for drapery and other details; these were then built up on the armature to provide the outer covering of the statue. Each piece had to be carefully matched to its neighbour, each join had to be carefully camouflaged, until the finished statue gave the appearance of a solid figure. The satirist Lucian in the second century AD could joke that the interior of the statue of Zeus at Olympia had become infested by mice, but these gold and ivory statues must have created an overpowering sense of richness and power, and such a medium provided the means to convey the majesty of Zeus.

Pheidias left no writings to tell us how he envisaged this daunting commission. At the Olympic games in AD 97 the orator Dio Chrysostom was invited to give a speech at the temple of Zeus and there he proclaimed, as if in the words of Pheidias himself, his view of how the sculptor had approached his subject. A story was current that when asked by his close relative and collaborator, Panaenus, how he conceived his figure of Zeus, Pheidias had quoted from the epic poet Homer, a passage in

29 *A Greek Imperial coin of Elis with the statue of Zeus at Olympia as its reverse type. (Florence Museum, from a cast)*

which he talks of an austere Zeus, the movement of whose head caused the whole of Mount Olympus to quake. Dio Chrysostom explains in rhetorical fashion the qualities that such a passage might evoke, and he lists the names by which Zeus was known: 'Father and king, Protector of cities, God of friendship and comradeship, Protector of suppliants, God of hospitality, Giver of increase . . .'. All these aspects of Zeus, he said, were to be found in the image, and it was precisely to underline the varied nature of the god that Pheidias chose to portray him as he did.

Cicero, that famous Roman orator of the first century BC, states that Pheidias 'had a vision of beauty in his mind so perfect that concentrating on it he could direct his artist's hand to produce a real likeness of the god'. Here was the king of the gods fashioned in a manner that conveyed every aspect of his godhead, a figure that produced awe in the hearts of those who believed that they were in the presence of Zeus himself. How was Pheidias able to achieve this?

The search for how this statue actually appeared in ancient times begins with the coins of neighbouring Elis (Figure 29), the city in which the architect Libon was born. It was fairly common for coins of the Greek world to depict a miniature representation of a well known statue and it is therefore no surprise to find that there are several occasions on which the great statue of Zeus provided inspiration for coin designs. Indeed, no other accurate representations exist, since apparently this remarkable statue did not lend itself to being copied on a small scale. However, beside the coins we do have a number of rich literary descriptions and we

30 *Reconstruction drawing of Pheidias' chyselephantine statue of Zeus. (After Swaddling)*

can therefore reconstruct the statue in considerable detail (Figure 30).

The geographer Strabo wrote early in the first century AD:

> The statue is made of ivory and it is of such size that although the temple itself is very large, the sculptor may be criticized for not having appreciated the correct proportions. He has shown Zeus seated, but with the head almost touching the ceiling, so that we have the impression that if Zeus moved to stand up, he would unroof the temple.

In Strabo's opinion the statue was too large to fit comfortably within the building and a Roman gem exists which shows Zeus in just such an uncomfortable composition (Figure 31).

We know the approximate measurements from a poem by Callimachus (305–240 BC) written nearly 200 years after the statue was made. Its overall length and breadth can also be

31 *Roman engraved carnelian ringstone with representation of the statue of Zeus at Olympia within its temple. (Cabinet des Médailles, Bibliothèque Nationale, Paris)*

measured on the floor of the excavated temple. The base was 6.65m wide, nearly 10m deep, and over a metre high. The statue itself was 13m high, as tall as a three-storey house, a gigantic figure that filled the west end of the temple and made his presence felt throughout the sanctuary.

For a detailed description of the statue we can turn to Pausanias, a Greek of the second century AD. He toured the Peloponnese writing as he went a guide to the monuments and buildings of the cities in which he stayed. He has left us a remarkable account of what he saw, sometimes difficult to interpret now that the cities are no more, but invaluable in allowing us to give names and descriptions to the broken foundations discovered by the excavators of a site such as Olympia.

Pausanias describes the statue of Zeus:

> On his head lies a sculpted wreath of olive sprays. On his right hand he holds a figure of Victory made from ivory and gold. . . . In his left hand the god holds his sceptre inlaid with every kind of metal, and the bird perched on the sceptre is an eagle. The sandals of the god are made of gold, as is his robe, and his garments are carved with animals and with lily flowers. The throne is decorated with gold and with precious stones, with ebony and with ivory.

In AD 174 a building to the west of the temple, just outside the main sanctuary wall, was pointed out to Pausanias as the

32 *View from the east end of the temple of Zeus at Olympia, its mosaic pavement in the foreground, along the length of the temple to the distant Byzantine church built on the foundations of Pheidias' workshop*

workshop of Pheidias, where the great statue had been created. The archaeological excavations by the German Archaeological Institute in 1958 proved in a dramatic manner that Pausanias' informant was correct (Figure 32). Two deposits of debris were found, literally rubbish dumps of material thrown out from this building. They were found to contain tools suitable for work on such a sculpture (Figure 33), discarded cores of ivory, fragments of metal and glass, and there were even terracotta moulds which had been used for the creation of drapery (Figure 34). The dumps could be dated to the 430s and later. There can be no doubt that this is the waste material from the workshop that created a 'chryselephantine' sculpture, a statue of gold and ivory, and that that sculpture was the image of Zeus by Pheidias. As if further confirmation was needed, the base of a broken jug was also found, inscribed in careful fifth-century BC letters, 'I belong to Pheidias' (Figure 35).

The statue itself cannot have been built entirely in this

33 Bronze tools found in the excavations of Pheidias' workshop. (Olympia Museum)

workshop and then transported to the temple, although the excavators at first thought that it was. The floor of the workshop simply would not have supported the enormous weight of the complete statue. The problem in the dismantling and transport of such a complicated structure must have been immense. Rather, pieces must have been planned and made in the workshop for final construction in the temple. The moulds show how small many of the sheets of precious metal must have been. Yet they were made with the close attention to detail that marks Pheidias' work on the Parthenon on the Acropolis at Athens.

Pausanias was an enthusiastic visitor. His eyes devoured the details of Pheidias' masterpiece and he has faithfully transcribed his notes for us. It was the throne that impressed him most, partly because Pheidias had lavished upon it all his skill in carving and partly, of course, because the throne was easier to see in the shadows of the interior of the temple. Although the building was roofed with marble tiles that would have been slightly translucent, the upper parts of the figure of Zeus were probably difficult to see in detail.

Winged figures of Victory, placed back to back, decorated the

34 *Terracotta mould for drapery details from the site of Pheidias' workshop. (Olympia Museum)*

legs of the throne, and figures of 'Theban children seized by sphinxes' were set above each of the two front legs. The sphinx, the monster with female head, lion's body and the wings of an eagle, used to kill the young men of Thebes in central Greece who could not answer the riddle 'what creature is two-footed, three-footed, and four-footed, and is weakest when it has most feet?' Close examination of the statue of Zeus depicted on one of the coins (Figure 29) shows that the arm rests are supported by the figure of a seated sphinx with its wing just below the elbow of Zeus. A clearer impression is given by a statue group found at Ephesos of a boy seized by the sphinx in just such a way as Pheidias must have sculpted.

Below the sphinx was placed a scene of the god Apollo and of his sister Artemis, shooting down with arrows poor Niobe and her children. Niobe had boasted that she surpassed in fertility Leto, the mother of Apollo and Artemis, and in this way she paid the price for her pride. This scene was carved along the sides of

35 *Base of an Athenian blackware cup with a scratched graffito reading 'I belong to Pheidias'. (Olympia Museum)*

the seat of the throne. A trace of it survives in a Red-Figure vase from Basky in South Russia, recently published, and it has been suggested that a later, Roman copy of a fifth-century BC original of this same theme might have derived from that of the statue of Zeus. Further echoes have been seen in several vases and reliefs (Figure 36). Apollo and Artemis were placed at the front of each side of the throne, shooting down the sides at the children of Niobe who were shown in the contorted postures of agony that were fashionable in the fifth century.

Pausanias' account is full of such details, showing the statue to be a veritable treasure house of Greek mythology. On the richly decorated strut that stretched between the front legs of the throne he noticed that one of the sculptures was missing. No one knew how it had disappeared. Another of the figures on the same strut 'placing the ribbon of victory in his hair, is said to be Pantarkes, a young lad from Elis who was the favourite of Pheidias. He won the boys' wrestling in the eighty-sixth Olympiad' (436 BC). Such

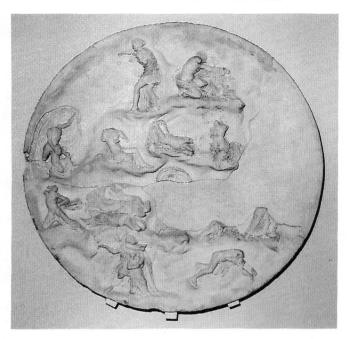

36 *Hellenistic circular marble tondo showing the slaughter of the children of Niobe by Apollo and Artemis. Its inspiration was probably the fifth-century frieze by Pheidias of the same subject on the throne of his statue of Zeus at Olympia. (British Museum)*

mention of Pantarkes tells us quite clearly when Pheidias was working at Olympia.

Another story, mentioned by the Christian writer Clement of Alexandria, stated that on the finger of Zeus was scratched the sentence 'Pantarkes is beautiful', a graffito with sexual overtones which suggests that the young Pantarkes was the lover of Pheidias. At all events, the stories that connect Pheidias with Pantarkes strongly corroborate the finds from the excavations of the workshop to show that it was after his flight from Athens that Pheidias worked on the statue of Zeus.

'On the other struts of the throne Herakles and his friends are shown in battle with the Amazons,' Pausanias continues with his description. There were, he says, 29 figures in two groups, emphasising that these struts were truly impressive pieces of

37 *Relief of Herakles and the battle of the Amazons from the temple of Apollo at Bassae. (British Museum)*

sculptural decoration. The theme of the battle between Herakles and the Amazons is that of the ninth of the hero's labours, set upon him by Eurystheus, king of Argos. He was sent to fetch for the king's daughter the golden girdle worn by Hippolyte, the queen of the Amazons, a race of warrior women who lived on the Black Sea coast. The ensuing battle is a favourite in early Greek sculpture and painting. A well known example is the frieze from the temple of Apollo at Bassae in Arcadia, not very far from Olympia, designed by the architect of the Parthenon at Athens, Ictinus. This frieze was sculpted *c.* 425 BC, at about the same time as the statue of Zeus, and the agitated movement and the swirling drapery of the contestants must also have been characteristic of Pheidias' finely carved work (Figure 37).

Pausanias comments upon four columns, in addition to the four legs of the throne, which gave it extra support. These do not appear on the miniature representations on the coins and it is possible that they were not part of Pheidias' original design. We can visualise them inside the throne, under the seat itself, which had to support the whole weight of the gigantic figure above.

Zeus held his long sceptre in his left hand. A winged figure of Victory, which itself would have been of no mean size, stood on his right hand, the weight supported by the arm rest of the throne. His feet rested on a large footstool the sides of which were in the form of standing lions, made of gold and, again, Pausanias comments on a scene of Amazons, this time accompanied by Theseus, the local hero of Athens. The great base that supported the statue itself was constructed in blue-black Eleusinian marble, richly decorated with relief figures in gold from the well known stories of Greek mythology: the sun-god Helios mounted in his chariot; Zeus and his queen, Hera; Eros welcoming Aphrodite, the goddess of love, as she rises from the sea; the moon mounted on a horse, and many other figures. The darker background of the stone highlighted the movement of the figures caught in a moment's stillness, a method of adding to the colour that was used on the friezes of the Erechtheum at Athens.

Perhaps the most dramatic element of Pausanias' description is his detailed account of the paintings by Panaenus which were on the screen walls preventing access to the throne. It is easy to forget that painting was as important an element of the artistic world in ancient times as it was in the Renaissance. The visitor to Pompeii or to the late Minoan Acrotiri on the island of Thera knows the dramatic effect of mural paintings in private houses. It is our misfortune that practically none has survived from the Greek world, so that it is difficult for us to share the excitement that such paintings aroused in ancient times.

Panaenus was one of the leading painters of his day. Pausanias calls him Pheidias' brother, Strabo his nephew. Whatever their relationship, they must have collaborated on many of Pheidias' major projects.

The screen walls showed nine scenes, probably painted as a sequence of separate pictures on either side of the throne. The back of the throne was protected by the wall of the building. There is no connecting theme in the pictures, but several of them were clearly chosen to reflect the architectural sculptures which decorated the exterior of the walls of the temple. Two refer to the sculptures which decorated the pediments – the triangular spaces between the gabled roof and the end walls. The marriage of Pirithous, the king of the Lapiths from Thessaly in northern Greece – himself said to be a son of Zeus – was the theme of the west pediment. The king had invited to the feast the Centaurs, wild creatures of the wooded mountain slopes, half horse and half man, who became drunk, assaulted the women and attempted to carry off Pirithous' bride. This theme had been used by Pheidias for the architectural slabs of sculpture, the metopes, on the outside of the Parthenon.

Another of Panaenus' pictures was of Hippodameia, whose connection with the foundation of the Olympic games has already been related. This theme was celebrated in the sculptures of the eastern pediment of the temple. The Labours of Herakles are illustrated in three of Panaenus' pictures and these too had been used by the architect for the subject of the frieze of sculptured plaques around the walls of the temple (Figure 38). Another story from the many legends about Herakles was placed by Panaenus next to the picture of Hippodameia. He showed Herakles going to the rescue of the Titan demi-god Prometheus, who was punished by Zeus for giving to mankind the use of fire. Prometheus was

38 *Herakles supporting the world on his shoulders for Atlas, who brings him the apples of the Hesperides whilst Athena looks on. Metope from the temple of Zeus at Olympia. -(Olympia Museum)*

chained to a rock and an eagle was sent to eat his liver which grew again at night as fast as the eagle could devour it by day. A picture such as this contrasts sharply with the orator Dio Chrysostom's theme of Zeus' 'gentleness and kindness', and must have reminded his fifth-century worshippers of the terrible power wielded by Zeus the thunderer.

One of the most interesting of Panaenus' paintings was a topical historical reference to the battle in which the Greeks of central and southern Greece united to defeat the mighty Persian empire. This was the sea battle off the island of Salamis near Athens in 480 BC, an event that had occurred only a few years before the building of the temple of Zeus at Olympia had begun. Panaenus had also painted a remarkable picture of the battle of Marathon in the famous 'Painted Stoa' in the market place at Athens. This was the battle in which the small army of the Athenians had prevented the landing of the much greater Persian army of Darius I in 490 BC and, like the battle of Salamis, was seen to be the defiant victory of the Greeks over the barbarian peoples of the east.

The paintings put the finishing touches to the great decorative statue of Zeus. It would seem that Pheidias survived to see his work completed, although he was in his fifties when it began. He is believed to have returned to Athens in 432 BC and there to have been murdered by his political opponents. If we are to assume that the entire work was completed in five years or so, we must also assume that Pheidias had a team of sculptors working with him, as he certainly had on the Parthenon sculptures at Athens.

> When the image was completely finished, Pheidias prayed to Zeus to show by a sign whether the work was to his liking. Immediately, so the story goes, a thunderbolt fell on the spot where to this day a bronze jar stands to cover the place. All the floor in front of the statue is paved with black marble, not white, edged in a semicircle by a raised rim of Parian marble, which acts as a basin for the olive oil that is poured over the statue.

So Pausanias ends his vivid description of the statue.

From the moment of its construction the statue was admired as the great masterpiece of the golden age of classical sculpture. The care of the statue was in the hands of the 'burnishers', said to be the descendants of Pheidias. The strange custom of pouring olive oil over it, remarked upon by Pausanias, may have arisen as a result of the serious cracking of the ivory that occurred in the damp conditions of the sanctuary. This was particularly bad in the middle of the second century BC and Damophon, a sculptor from the city of Messene to the south, was called in to mend the statue. This he is said to have done most skillfully; it may have been at this time that four columns were placed under the seat in order to prevent it collapsing under the great weight of the figure above.

At about the same time, in 167 BC, Antiochus IV King of Syria, dedicated in the temple of Zeus a woollen curtain 'adorned with Assyrian woven patterns and Phoenician die'. This curtain of Near Eastern origin probably hung at the back of the statue and it was of sufficient importance to be commented upon by Pausanias. It was this same Antiochus who despoiled the Temple of Solomon at Jerusalem and gave orders that it should be renamed the temple of Olympian Zeus. Amongst the treasures that Antiochus seized from the Temple must have been the great veil that stretched across the interior. It does not require much imagination to assert that this was the very curtain that Antiochus dedicated to the king of his gods at Olympia.

The statue continued to attract the awe and wonder of those who believed in Zeus. Over 450 years after it was made, the Roman emperor Caligula (AD 37–41), in the tradition of those Roman conquerors who robbed the Greek world of its art treasures, set his heart on having the statue in Rome. Craftsmen were dispatched to contrive a means to transport it, but the statue 'suddenly emitted such a cackle of laughter that the scaffolding collapsed and the workmen fled'. Suetonius, Caligula's biographer, enjoyed relating this story of the emperor that he loved to hate, but the statue could not remain inviolate for ever. In AD 391 the triumphant clergy of the Christian church persuaded the emperor Theodosius I to ban the practice of pagan cults and to close the temples. The Olympic games ceased and the great sanctuary of Olympia fell into disuse.

The cult statue, by this time over 800 years old, was at last transported from its temple to adorn a palace in Constantinople. The workshop of Pheidias was turned into a Christian church. The temple itself was severely damaged by fire about 425 and, in the sixth century AD the river Alphaeus changed its course. The whole area of Olympia, untended, was destroyed by landslides, earthquakes and floods. For over a thousand years the site lay covered by a thick deposit of sand, mud and debris. The removal of the statue to Constantinople had saved it from these disasters, but in AD 462 there was a severe fire in Constantinople itself, which destroyed the palace in which the statue of Zeus was housed. While the sanctuary at Olympia was crumbling with neglect in the Peloponnese, this remarkable statue, held to be the greatest work of classical sculpture, was destroyed on the shores of the Bosporus.

No copies of the statue have survived to show us in better detail how it appeared. At Cyrene, in Libya, a very large copy served as the cult statue of the local temple of Zeus. The base of this has been found in the excavations, but no more. Sculptors appear to have been strangely reluctant to copy, even as a small statuette, the great work of Pheidias. We are fortunate indeed to be able to share through the writings of such authors as Pausanias the impression made by the statue. Had it stayed in Olympia, stripped perhaps of the precious metals, it is possible that some fragments would have survived for us to admire today.

THE TEMPLE OF ARTEMIS AT EPHESOS

BLUMA L. TRELL

IN AD 1780, Edward Gibbon mournfully recorded the destruction in AD 262 of the temple of Artemis at Ephesos by the Ostrogoths. His eloquent description of the monument, sight unseen, is among the most elegant ever written:

> The arts of Greece and the wealth of Asia had conspired to erect that sacred and magnificent structure. . . . Successive empires, the Persian, the Macedonian and the Roman revered its sanctity and enriched its splendour.

Gibbon depended on the stories, historical and mythological, written by the Greeks and Romans, which he knew very well. He also knew about the celebrated Wonders of the World. He was born, however, a century too early to know the wonders of archaeology. Even with his educated intuition, he did not anticipate that the temple which he believed was gone forever would some day be found.

No historian, historiographer or psychologist has ever been able to explain satisfactorily why it never occurred to anyone before the nineteenth century to dig beneath the earth to find a lost monument (Figure 39). The very first venture of this kind in the Hellenic world took place in the watery plain near the mouth of the Cayster river in Ephesos. In the 1860s, for seven years, a compatriot of Gibbon's, John Turtle Wood, dug in the alluvial mud until he came upon a foundation block of a column of a temple (Figure 40). Wood's pioneering work preceded the discovery of Troy in 1870 by Schliemann. Wood was followed almost continuously by other archaeologists. Now, approximately one hundred years later, Anton Bammer of the Austrian

39 *View of the present site of the temple of Artemis at Ephesos. The site is heavily waterlogged and the single column has been re-erected in recent years*

Archaeological Institute is still bringing forth wonders from the bowels of the sacred earth of the goddess Artemis, the Diana of the Ephesians.

It was the magnificent architecture of the great sanctuary of Artemis that won it a place in the canon of the Seven Wonders. 'Graecae magnificae' are the words used by Pliny the Elder to describe the temple and he was no less an historian than Gibbon. The Greek temple has been characterised as the house of the soul, different from the Egyptian temple, which was the house of the god, and the cathedral, the house of the people. The temple of Artemis could be described as an expression of Greek Ionic soul, but mixed in large measure with Near Eastern oriental spirit.

The Artemisium was more than a simple, over-sized, rectangular edifice surrounded on all sides by a colonnade (Figure 41). It was a vast gleaming marble building in a great courtyard open to the skies to be viewed from afar. For the view of the façade it was necessary to retreat as far back as the altar court, otherwise the decorated pediment could not be seen because it was so high up.

The altar court itself, decorated with columns and statues, was positioned at a distance and directly in the line of view of the centre of the façade. The small sacrificial altar within the altar court was, however, set asymmetrical. The priest involved in a ceremonial ritual could see the high places of the temple but he was obliged to turn away to attend to the small sacrificial altar (Figure 42). This arrangement is reminiscent of the Near East where temples were sometimes entered from the side, not front portals, or inner sacred rooms were approached by oblique passageways.

Access to the high terrace of the temple was by means of marble steps built around the whole building like a giant frame with receding mouldings or embrasures laid flat on the ground. The high platform was approximately 78.5m (255ft) wide and 131m (425ft) long. Pliny tells us that the columns were 20m (60ft) high, slender and beautifully fluted. Their elaborate bases

40 *The first sight of columns from the lost temple of Artemis at Ephesos, rescued from the bottom of the Cayster river in the 1860s. (Engraving published by J.T. Wood)*

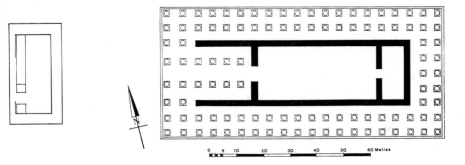

41 *Ground plan of the late classical temple of Artemis at Ephesos and its altar court. Although many columns have not yet been found, the plan established a total number reported by the Roman writer, Pliny the Elder. (After Bammer)*

consisted of mouldings like rings of marble supporting sculptured reliefs that 'ran around' the bottom drums, an architectural delight almost but not entirely without precedent in the ancient world. Exquisite Ionic capitals with their expertly and gracefully carved circular sides (volutes) protected the columns and supported the marble horizontal beam above (entablature). There were no figures on the frieze but huge dentils made up the very top moulding, supporting the triangular space above. In the pediment were three prominent openings or windows; the one in the centre was furnished with doors. Framing the centre door were the statues of two Amazons, with two more in the eaves. Antefixes decorated the roof.

Perhaps more dramatic than the view of the façade with its 'storied' drums was the sight that greeted the visitor as he entered between the central columns. Here, in front of the porch, was a 'forest of columns' resting on sculptured rectangular bases. These were matched by another 'forest' in the rear porch of the temple. Pliny counts 127 columns in all. In order to 'fit' this large number onto the ground plan, the modern archaeologist was obliged to propose nine columns for the rear façade. The cella or house of the goddess stood in the near centre of the edifice, backed and fronted by the two porches of columns. We have no proof that the cult statue of Artemis Ephesia dominated the sacred room, as did the statues of Athena at Athens or that of Zeus in the sanctuary at Olympia. We may speculate, however, that the cult

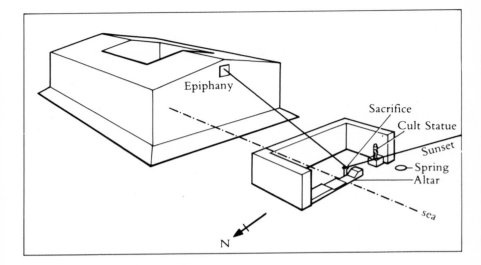

42 *Sketch of the religious ceremony carried out before the temple of Artemis. The priest performs at a sacrificial altar in the altar court as he directs his attention to a divine appearance in the pedimental window of the temple. (After Bammer)*

statue of Artemis Ephesia was the size of the Roman copies erected in the courtyard in the time of the Roman empire. With their elaborate crowns, they were considerably taller than life-size.

The fame of the temple of Artemis was also due to the extraordinary dramatis personae who played important parts in the religious and political life of the city. The goddess herself played her role whenever she was needed, like a *deus ex machina* of a Greek drama by Euripides. She is reported to have helped the architect, Chersiphron, set up the lintel over the entrance way of the great marble temple, unromantically called temple D by the archaeologists. So enormous and heavy was the stone beam that the architect considered suicide when contemplating his task.

From the earliest times, Artemis attracted pilgrims and tourists, earning the income for her temple from them and from the ships that used her sacred port. She shared in the profits made by merchants who frequented her open courtyard: artisans who sold miniature silver copies of her cult statue and temple, fortune-telling magicians who sold oracles, and priests and priestesses who sold parts of the sacrificial meat. Broken bones of animals were found in the sanctuary indicating that the food eaten there was hot off the altars. Artemis came to the rescue of Croesus, the last Lydian king who had helped to build the monumental temple (D) in her honour: a Sibyl intervened with Cyrus the Great, the conquering Persian king, at the very moment in 546 BC when he was sacrificing Croesus on a pyre.

The goddess herself failed to intervene when disaster threatened her sanctuary. The Croesus building (D) was burnt to the ground by a man named Herostratus who thereby hoped to make his name immortal. This weird character ironically made a contribution to world history: 'Herostratan' became a synonym for the word 'infamous'. For Plutarch, writing in the second century AD, Herostratus provided an opportunity to make a good story better. The goddess, wrote Plutarch, was too busy taking care of the birth of Alexander the Great which occurred on the very night of the fire (21 July 356) to send help to her threatened temple.

Alexander the Great was only twenty-two when he came as victor to Ephesos. He knew that only a few years before a statue of his father Philip II had been set up in the newly restored temple of Artemis (called E by the archaeologists). He also knew that Croesus' name in Greek and Lydian had been inscribed on the decorated columns of the earlier temple (D). He would certainly have known that contributions to a building entitled the donor to an honorific plaque. He tried to ingratiate himself with the Ephesians, supplying a sacrifice and procession for a festival in honour of Artemis. But when he offered to pay for the completion of the temple on condition that his name be inscribed on the building, a diplomatic and discreet citizen suggested to him that it was not fitting for one god to make gifts to another.

The law of asylum of the temple of Artemis added to its fame and to its treasury. Like many ancient temples it served a dual capacity in being a banking as well as a religious institution. Of all the suppliants who sought sanctuary at the temple, the most fascinating were the legendary Amazons. Their request for asylum must have been granted since they gained the reputation, amongst others, as founders of the temple and their statues were set up within the pediment (Figure 43). The generally accepted historical founder of the first monumental marble temple (D) was Croesus, the Lydian king. During an armed struggle between him and a nephew, the Ephesians tied a rope from the endangered Acropolis to one of the columns of the temple and thus provided asylum to the entire city. Later in the sixth century a brutal tyrant, Pythagoras, unable to capture a young woman, kept her imprisoned in the temple, where she had fled for sanctuary. Unfortunately, she hanged herself in desperation. The Persian king Xerxes, after he was defeated by the Greeks, sent his children to the temple of Artemis. There they were guarded by one of the most colourful women in Greek history, Queen Artemisia, who took part as an admiral in the sea battle against the Greeks.

Alexander the Great showed his well-known intemperate character by following the rules of sanctuary in one case, politely asking the chief priest for a fugitive slave, and breaking the rules when he had two suppliants removed by force to face death by stoning. In one of the tragedies of the Egyptian Ptolemies, Ptolemy Physcon, half-brother of Ptolemy Euergetes, fled in 259 BC with his consort Eirene to the asylum of the temple, where they were both murdered. In another tragedy, Marc Antony forced the chief priest to bring out of the temple the sister of Cleopatra, Arsinoe. He then murdered her, thus assuring Cleopatra (and himself) the throne of Egypt.

The temple of Artemis also attracted philosophers, poets and artists. The sixth-century BC philosopher Heracleitus compelled himself to take up sacred residence in the sanctuary to escape, it is said, not men but mankind. Chersiphron, the troubled architect of the early temple (D) mentioned above, had the help not only of the goddess but also of his architect son, Metagenes, and that of a third architect, Theodoros, who, we can assume, had already experienced similar structural problems at nearby Samos. Praxiteles, the famous sculptor, fashioned statues for the altar of the Croesus temple (D) and the later Scopas decorated the column bases of the late classical building (E).

Of all the contests held by the Greeks, in athletics, poetry, plays, music, the contest in sculptural art in the fifth century BC was in many respects unique. Sculptors were invited to exhibit their bronze statues of Amazons. Four statues judged the best (they were by the sculptors Pheidias, Polycleitus, Kresilas and Phradmon) were chosen to decorate temple D. This artistic event was held to celebrate the Peace of Callias in 450 BC as well as the

43 (*Opposite*) *A typical Roman copy of the classical statues of the Amazons which decorated the pediment of the temple of Artemis. This example is possibly after an original by Polycleitus. (Capitoline Museum, Rome)*

completion of the Croesus temple. No better symbol than the Amazons could have been chosen to celebrate a conflict between east and west. Amazons were not an army of fighting women with one breast. They symbolised some Eastern peoples, perhaps the belligerent priestesses of Ma, an oriental mother-goddess of east Anatolia, or an invading army of Hittites, or some other peripheral tribes of the east. Represented on the temple in the fifth century BC (Figure 43), they symbolised the Persians who came from the east and seized the temple after defeating the Lydians.

In the first century AD St Paul came from Corinth to Ephesos, a rich and flourishing city. Ancient writers describe the oriental luxury, the golden pillars, the paintings by artists in the temple, yet ancient critics describe the city as full of bordellos, singers, actors, playboys and whores. The well-known confrontation between Paul and the crowd goaded by Demetrius the silversmith took place not in the temple but in the theatre. When St Paul spoke against the silver idols, the crowd made its hostile feelings known by shouting 'Great is Diana of the Ephesians' (Acts 19: 24–34). That St Paul was shocked by the vulgarity of Artemis' cult image can certainly be assumed. A vivid description of the cult image comes from another saintly man (or men?), John, who also visited Ephesos in the first century AD. John is reported to have had more success with the crowd than Paul, but the truth is the Ephesians did not forsake Artemis until the end of the fourth century AD. As John walked about the city he saw a painted statue of Artemis with gilded lips and a veil over her face. He also visited the theatre during the festival of the goddess where the sacrificial smoke was so thick that it veiled the sun. He had a good view of the procession with the priests blowing horns as it moved to the temple.

British archaeologists discovered an inscription, to be dated after the visits of the saints, which provides a splendid portrayal of a procession in honour of Artemis. A benefactor, C. Vibius Salutaris, provided for a procession in a festival in honour of Artemis' birthday. It seems as though the whole city of Ephesos took part, administrators, magistrates, priests and priestesses of the temple, musicians, dancers, young people, some carrying instruments for the sacrifice, others leading animals to the sacrifice, some people on horseback and, most important, others carrying statues of the goddess. The main purpose of the procession was to carry the cult image of the goddess out of the temple in order that she might attend the performance in the theatre, consisting mainly of games and then, on the return, to watch the sacrifices in the sanctuary. Artemis Ephesia was epiphanes, a divinity who 'appeared' in order that her worshippers could behold and revere her. She might take a place in a sacred window or be transported in a processional vehicle, a kind of chariot. This ritualistic appearance of the goddess is an Oriental convention centuries-old in Anatolia, Syria, Mesopotamia and Egypt. High in the gable of the temple Artemis had a large opening at which she could be seen by the worshippers below. Such a 'window of appearance' came from the temples of Phrygia, an empire which lost its power when it lost its last king, Midas (c. 700 BC), but the influence of its religious ritual was handed down from generation to generation.

The Phrygians also worshipped a goddess who made a ritual appearance, Cybele, the great mother-goddess. She emerged from the stone mountainsides; sometimes, although she had no visible form, she was present in the stone itself. At other times she was represented as a stone pillar protected by her lions or in human form between her animals. A niche framing her carved in the natural rock virtually made a window of appearance. Two such windows are actually carved in a temple pediment in the rock, each window enclosing a celestial symbol. Artemis Ephesia had almost the same attributes as the mother-goddess of Phrygia, Kybele. In fact, Artemis was named Kubaba (Cybele) in several Anatolian dialects. The frequent use in the Greek of megale–, great–, with her name suggests she was *magna mater*, the great mother-goddess, and in this the great goddess of Ephesos differs from the huntress goddess of purely Greek mythology. Her origins lie in the east, not in Greece itself.

The peculiar many-breasted statue of Artemis Ephesia represents a mother goddess, the breasts symbolising the fertility of woman (Figure 44). The statue is rigid, the lower portion like an Egyptian mummy case. The decorative elements, stags, bulls, lions, griffins, sphinxes, sirens and bees, are creatures originally of the east. Scholarly curiosity has produced strange questions: are the breasts really breasts? Or are they palm-dates, acorns, eggplant, ostrich-eggs, scrotum of bull, bags to hold amulets or other decorations? The correct answer, if it were possible to arrive at one, does not help to solve a more important problem. There is no doubt that the polymaste Artemis was the cult image from

44 *Statue of the goddess Artemis, a Roman copy of the cult statue worshipped in the temple of Ephesos. Artemis displayed her nature as a great mother-goddess in the elaborate decorations added to her rigid form. (Museo Nazionale, Naples)*

about the third century BC until the temple was destroyed by the Goths in the third century AD. The question is: what was the cult image before that time?

In the so-called Foundation Deposit (*c.* 600 BC) of the earliest level in the excavation area were found primitive-looking, rigidly-formed statuettes made of gold, wood, ivory or clay. Legendary stories have come down about early cult images in the form of a branch, a tree or a stone fallen from the heavens. Xenophon said he saw a golden *xoanon* figure in the temple, a primitive statue similar in form to the figures found in the excavations. The archaic figurines of the Foundation Deposit show a delightful mélange of Oriental features, Lydian, Persian, Phrygian, Hittite, Assyrian, Egyptian. Some believe they represent the early cult image. Others see priestesses in some of the figurines. One of these which until recently was considered a priest is now identified as a priestess, so great is the problem.

A clue to the identity of the early figurines comes from the inscription of Salutaris. Some of the statues which this generous citizen ordered to be set up in the sanctuary were not the many-breasted image; they were representations of Artemis as the Huntress goddess with the bow and as goddess of the underworld with a torch. We know for certain that the cult image was not changed in the second century AD: the coins of the Roman Imperial period clearly display the many-breasted Artemis. The statues ordered by Salutaris did not (nor were they intended to) represent the cult image of the sanctuary, as some have assumed. They represent different aspects of the deity more agreeable to the changing population of the Graeco-Roman period than that of the Oriental goddess. Like these Roman statues, the archaic figurines showed different aspects of the goddess in the sixth century BC. The goddess with spindle and with falcon, for example, comes close to Kubaba (Cybele) the Hittite-Phrygian-Syrian *magna mater*. The connection with Phrygia is underlined by two Phrygian *fibulae* (pins) that were found in the area of the Croesus temple.

Even more important for the identity of the cult image in the early period is the fact that the late classical temple (E) is similar in design and other details to the Croesus building (D). Why did the Ephesians decide to retain the appearance of the lost temple and even preserve some drums from its broken columns below the raised platform of the new building? In Athens, the defeated Greeks buried the statues and buildings that were damaged by the Persians so that they were completely hidden, and built an entirely new complex of sacred buildings above. In Rome, after an earthquake destroyed the great temple of the Capitol (Figure 83), a law required that the new temple of Jupiter be an exact copy of the one that had been damaged. Today it has become the practice to preserve as a visible memorial some part of the destruction, as at Coventry and Hiroshima. The Ephesians obviously took great care to imitate the earlier temple. It is difficult to accept the theory that they introduced an absolutely new type of cult image. Such a change seems more impious than altering the style of architecture.

Until better evidence is available, it is more reasonable to assume that there was no change of image in the fourth century. The investigation of the sanctuary is still going on today. It is believed that in the seventh and early part of the sixth centuries the sanctuary consisted of an altar-like structure at the west end which was changed several times (called A-B-C) and of two other monuments, the Hecatompedon, a hundred-foot structure, and the Ramp altar, at the east end. All of these were covered by the construction of the D temple by 550 BC and of an altar-court by 500 BC, the latter being an elaboration of the earlier Ramp altar. The sacred area with its altar-like structures open to the skies was similar to early cult-places of the Oriental world, particularly Semitic shrines. Here, often, there were no cult images because the altars were considered the dwelling place of the divinity, and thus the focus itself of worship. That may have been the situation in the earliest period at Ephesos.

Because the early shrines at the east end of the sanctuary faced east and those of the west end faced north, some believe that more than one cult was celebrated in the sanctuary, even as many as eight deities. It is more reasonable to assume only two, the related cults of Artemis and Cybele, who later by syncretism became one goddess with a dual nature, Artemis. It is a common phenomenon in the Near East that Graeco-Roman gods imposed themselves on the Oriental. At Baalbek, for example, the Jupiter who occupied the main temple was a Roman version of the native Semitic god, Hadad, just as he was of the Greek god. In Alexandria, in one and the same temple, there was a deity with a dual nature, Sarapis/Zeus Helios. It is no coincidence that the Baalbek Jupiter had a cult image and temple similar in some respects to the cult image and temple at Ephesos.

It would be misleading to ignore the great difference of opinion that exists among scholars, not only about the cult image and the archaic figures but also about dates, ground plans and elevations of the sanctuary. Bammer charmingly suggests the need for a firmly dated inscription. Given the difficulties of digging in metres of mud, and the disappearance of portions of the temple into churches and mosques at Ephesos and even into buildings in

45 *Coins of Ephesos struck in Roman times showing the statue of Artemis and her temple. Centre: a bronze coin of Maximus (AD 235–238). Note the detail of the pediment with its four sculpted figures of Amazons framing three windows. Below: silver cistophoric tetradrachms minted in the reigns of Claudius (AD 41–54) and Hadrian (AD 117–138). Both show the statue of Artemis which is also known from Hellenistic copies. The central window of the pediment seen on the coin of Claudius played a part in the ritual performed at the sanctuary (see Figure 42). Part of an ancient window frame was discovered in an early Christian building at Ephesos*

Constantinople (Istanbul), it is no wonder that more problems have been raised and remain unsolved since the discovery of the remains of the famous temple than existed before.

It is surprising how belatedly the best evidence for the appearance of the façade of the temple was recognised. The great temple (E) appears on coins that were minted in Ephesos at the very time when the sacred building was standing, intact and in use during the first three centuries AD (Figure 45). The evaluation of the evidence was made by such architectural historians as Bernard Ashmole, Karl Lehmann, Hugh Plommer, William Dinsmoor and

46 *Reconstruction of the late classical temple of Artemis with a line-drawing of a coin in an engraving by Johann Fischer von Ehrlach, 1721. The porch of four columns is based on a misunderstanding of the coin types*

Charles Picard. In one of the few instances where the coins were considered before the twentieth century, only one coin was used in the reconstruction of the temple. Not realising that the coin, which shows only four columns on the façade, was an abbreviation of the correct number, eight, shown on other coins, the eighteenth-century artist produced what looked like a church with a four-columned porch (Figure 46). Even today, the convention of abbreviation, well-known and acceptable in all other forms of art, seems to trouble some scholars.

It is not only the abbreviation that puzzled them but also what seemed to be arbitrary differences on the coins that represented the same building. A full appreciation of the die-makers' art makes it clear that the monument must be considerably abbreviated to be accommodated on a miniature coin-picture. It is also inevitable that different die-makers representing the same building would choose different details of the monuments to emphasise.

Fortunately, no one has questioned the importance of the coins discovered in the so-called 'foundation deposit'. They play an important part in another of the temple's problems – the date of

47 *Sculptured column drum from the late classical temple of Artemis at Ephesos. Contemporary coins establish that such decorated drums formed the lower course of the columns of the façade and were not set on great rectangular pedestals as suggested by some early writers. (British Museum)*

the very earliest building on the site. In the foundation of the Croesus building (D) were found 87 of the earliest coins known, many in the foundation deposit itself. There are still questions about the actual date of the deposit, but it must certainly fall no earlier than 625 and possibly as late as 575 BC. It is clear that there can have been no great temple on the site prior to that built under Croesus.

The architectural coins show that sculptured drums decorated the bottom of the façade columns (Figure 45). We are fortunate to have the evidence of Pliny who reports that 36 of the columns were decorated with sculpture (called *columnae caelatae*), a most unusual feature for a Greek temple. The excavations produced round sculptured drums (Figure 47) and rectangular sculptured bases belonging to both great temples, D and E, but Pliny did not indicate where the sculpted pieces were positioned. A surprising suggestion was made recently that the sculptured drums were not at the bottom but at the top of the columns, as decoration of the 'neck' immediately below the capitals. As supporting evidence was cited a decorated drum recently found in the excavation of the temple of Apollo Smintheus at Alexandria Troas. In that case a very small section of a fluted column was found attached to the underside of the drum; this would indicate that the drum was positioned above, not below the column. But the coins of Alexandria Troas, like those of Ephesos, show the drums at the base of the columns. It must also be pointed out that there is no evidence as to when the fluted column fragment was attached to the drum; it may have happened long after the temple was in ruins. It is hard to believe that the architect, Chersiphron, who worried about the weight on the columns, would have added to the pressure by placing the heavy drums above. Some believe that the pediment was pierced by three openings in order to relieve the weight on the columns. The convention of placing decorated bases below the columns (found earlier amongst the Hittites), is paralleled by a later use at Ephesos in the sixth century AD when similar decorated drums were placed at the bottom of the columns of the Arcadiane.

The outflange of the steps of the platform seen on the coins can be interpreted as indicating the presence of columns on all four sides. Evidence was discovered for a colonnade with a double row of columns on the sides. To accommodate the 127 columns described by Pliny, rows of columns were proposed in addition to the colonnade, in the porches and inner halls, front and back. The correct number of columns and the position of all of them is questioned, but there is no doubt that the Artemision was the second earliest example in the ancient Hellenic world (preceded only by the temple of Samos), of the use of what is described as a forest of columns. There can be no doubt that the forest of columns was inspired by the great temples of Egypt which Chersiphron, who came from Crete, could have easily known and brought to Ephesos in the sixth century BC.

The Ionic capitals found in the excavations are shown on the coins. These are also eastern in origin, a development from the earlier type, the Protoaeolic, examples of which have been found in Israel. An early ivory disk, recently discovered in Ephesos, is decorated with palmette-volutes, one of the acknowledged steps in the historical development from Aeolic capitals to Ionic. Because of other finds, fragments of decorated reliefs, etc., a continuous figured frieze has been suggested for the D temple and a frieze that includes lion-head spouts for the E temple. Some of the coins picture cornices with conspicuous dental mouldings, a convention legitimised by rock-cut monuments near Ephesos. Other coins show a moulding like a string of beads on the architrave which may represent the frieze suggested for the D temple. Some of the decorated reliefs may have belonged to the altar court. Later famous altar courts were certainly modelled after the Ephesos monument, such as the Zeus altar at Pergamum and the Ara Pacis at Rome, and they were also decorated with sculptured relief.

The coins indicate that the temple was roofed and had a decorated pediment (Figure 45). Vitruvius wrote that un-roofed temples (hypaethral) were constructed with ten columns front and back. By his definition, the Artemision, which had eight columns on the main façade and, apparently, nine at the back, was not hypaethral, yet some scholars propose that the temple was open to the rains; a drain drawing off water was found in the cella area. On the other hand, the discovery of clay roof tiles and water spouts implies that the temple was roofed. Another solution for the roof was offered for temple E: a truncated roof covering only the surrounding colonnade, slightly pitched and ending in gables or pediments; in other words, with a centre section open to the sky. A wooden roof was suggested for the Croesus temple (D). Some scholars could not conceive of a conflagration powerful enough to burn so much marble without sufficient timber. They even suggested the wooden roof was decorated with hanging fabrics. It is obvious that they did not consider Pliny's mention of a wooden stairway that led to the roof, thus providing an ideal passage for the fire to flare up through the building. Others could not conceive of the conflagration under any circumstances: no man could commit such a crime! The story of Herostratus' destruction of the temple in 356 BC, it was theorised, was an aetiological and romantic fabrication for a real, violent conflict with neighbouring Carians who could have easily destroyed the temple in a fire. The object of many ancient wars was to destroy the enemy's main edifice (a modern example of this is the firing of the White House in Washington in 1812). The trouble with this theory is that there is no evidence of a Carian invasion. More important, the Carians were ruled at that time by Maussollos whose affection for and admiration of the Greeks would make such an attack as inconceivable as the crime of Herostratus.

That the temple had pediments pierced by openings or windows is confirmed by the coins, by a fragment of the tympanum found in the ruins and a section of a window frame found in the church of St John. The windows pictured on the coins of Ephsos are exactly like those on the coins of Magnesia where there is even more archaeological evidence for the convention. The goddess of Magnesia was also epiphanes, like Artemis Ephesia. For many centuries numismatic publications described the windows as tables or altars; one amazingly perspicacious numismatist of the sixteenth century guessed right and drew them as windows.

Two examples of the Ephesos coin series show a female figure making a ritualistic appearance in the central window of the pediment. In one, the figure looks like Artemis Ephesia, in the other, the figure is more like that of a priestess. There is a very similar priestess who stands before a small shrine of Ephesian Artemis on the scene wall of the Roman theatre of Hierapolis, a city not far from Ephesos. A drawing offered by Bammer demonstrates the ritualistic use of the temple window *vis-à-vis* the altar court which had unusually high columns and an atypical entrance, as if the altar had little relationship with the temple. At Baalbek, the window of appearance must have served a similar ceremony. The tall altar – it was more like an independent shrine – blocked the view of the façade of the temple from most places in the courtyard.

The window-pediment, Oriental in origin, continued throughout the Christian period right up to the present. A thirteenth-century French manuscript shows St John destroying the temple and the statue of Artemis (Figure 48). The temple has been metamorphosed into a medieval Christian building but the windows still remain. In Romanesque Spain, on the west entrance of the church of St Vincent in Avila, there is an amazing miniature of an authentic classical temple with columns and with three windows in the pediment. Echoes of Ephesos are found in the bull-headed Persian capitals in the middle of the entrance, a type

a cum le temple od uic lcſ ydleſ chei par la preure ſanc iohan.

a cu ſanc iohan arraſunc ariſtodimc. e cu ariſtodimc demaunde deiſ

48 *French manuscript of the thirteenth century AD showing St John destroying the temple of Artemis at Ephesos. The medieval artist has faithfully recorded the three prominent windows of the ancient pediment. (Trinity College Library, Cambridge)*

of capital that was found in the excavations of several buildings at Ephesos and at Greek colonies in Spain. A famous legend says that a copy of the cult image of Artemis and of her temple was brought to Marseilles and from there to sister temples in Greek colonies in Spain. It hardly seems realistic to assume that the echoes from ancient Ephesos could directly persist until the twelfth century AD in Spain. However, there is a fascinating historical link between Spain and Ephesos in the medieval period. As early as the eleventh century, Crusaders from Spain travelled to the Near East and, in the thirteenth century, a Spanish group called the Catalan Grand Company actually ruled in Ephesos. Through these pilgrims the architectural conventions of Ephesos and of the famed temple of Artemis could have come to Spain, via manuscript illuminations or woven into oriental textiles.

The unique evidence that four female statues decorated the pediment is found on the coins. The manner in which they frame the windows is in the Oriental tradition of some beautiful monuments carved in the natural rock of ancient Turkey. It is no coincidence that the figures are four in number and female. The prize-winning statues destined for the temple were four in number and represented the female fighting Amazons. Here, however, they are shown in their role as suppliants seeking sanctuary within the temple. Their presence on the coins of the Imperial Roman period which represent temple E confirms the fact that E was made in the image of D. It was on the D-temple that the statues were placed in 450 BC.

One detail of the reconstruction, the gorgon head, is to be accepted on circumstantial evidence. The gorgon appears in the early temple of Corfu. It occupies exactly the same place as on the temple coins on an early relief from Locris, Italy. Gorgon heads are mentioned as among the precious pieces taken from the temple area which Justinian sent to Constantinople (Istanbul) in the sixth century AD. At this time, the temple of Artemis was no longer extant. After the Goths destroyed it in AD 262 some rebuilding was undertaken at the end of the third century but the use of the building was hardly tolerated in the fourth century. In AD 401 it was completely destroyed by St John Chrysostom. Legend has it that people still worshipped at stones taken from the sacred area. The very earliest, most sacred, image was said to be a stone fallen from the heavens, probably a meteor. Worshipping stones was not strange. Many of the sister goddesses of Artemis Ephesia looked quite like stones. Artemis of Perga, for example, as shown on the coins of that city, is no more than a slab of stone with a head. Besides stones, thanks to the image of Ephesos on the coins, the pagan could continue to worship at his temple in their hands right up to the advent of Christianity.

In the centuries that followed, Ephesos had its ups and downs, nothing more down than the temple under the mud of ages. By the seventeenth century Ephesos was a deserted, poverty-stricken, squalid village, but the temple of Artemis was not completely lost to humankind. The many-breasted statue of Artemis Ephesia of Naples and similar statues have survived to this day. They served as models for Raphael's paintings in the Vatican in the sixteenth century and for Tiepolo's paintings in the eighteenth century. A sculptured copy made for the Villa d'Este at Tivoli in the sixteenth century was still there at the time of the Second World War. The architectural elevation of the temple of Ephesos, reconstructed on the basis of the coins and published after the Second World War, served as a model for the contemporary painter, Salvador Dali. He made an exact facsimile of the elevation

49 *Painting by Salvador Dali entitled* The Temple of Diana at Ephesus,
*1952. The artist adopts the reconstruction of the temple made on the basis of the
coins (see Figure 45). (Courtesy of Staempfli Gallery, New York)*

and added some dancing devotees of the goddess Artemis (Figure
49).

Shakespeare has preserved the memory of Ephesos for all ages
since neither the poet nor the temple of Artemis, in Horace's
immortal prediction, can ever entirely die. *The Comedy of Errors*
was admittedly a copy of Plautus' play but instead of using the
Latin poet's Greek town of Epidamnus, Shakespeare, poet that he
was, made his rich, sophisticated, metropolitan characters entangle
and disentangle themselves in the city of Ephesos. Why did he
make this change? Because he knew that Ephesos was one of the
richest banking centres of the ancient world, with a magnificent
temple that was truly one of the Wonders of the World.

THE MAUSOLEUM
AT HALICARNASSUS

GEOFFREY B. WAYWELL

THE MAUSOLEUM at Halicarnassus was the great tomb monument of Maussollos, who was ruler of Caria from 377 to 353 BC, and at the same time Satrap or Governor for the King of Persia, within whose empire his kingdom lay. So vast was the building's size by ancient standards and so lavish its sculptured decoration that it soon came to be considered one of the Seven Wonders of the Ancient World. By Roman times Mausoleum had become a generic term for any large built tomb, and remains so today. Maussollos was the son of Hekatomnos of Mylasa and, at some time during his reign, he moved his capital from there to the coastal city of Halicarnassus, marrying his sister Artemisia. It is Artemisia who is credited by ancient writers with the construction of the Mausoleum for her brother/husband and for that reason it has often been dated to the two-year period between his death and hers, 353–351 BC. But it is evident that the tomb was too large to have been planned and completed in this short space of time and it is more likely that it was begun during Maussollos' lifetime, perhaps soon after his refounding of Halicarnassus *c.* 370–365 BC, and that it was completed around 350 BC, shortly after Artemisia's death.

Ancient Halicarnassus is modern Bodrum in south-west Turkey, its harbour now dominated by a massive Crusader castle built by the Knights of St John of Malta in the fifteenth century (Figure 50). The site of the Mausoleum occupied a level area somewhat raised up above the harbour and is now close by a mosque.

In recent years the site has been completely cleared by excavation, but its appearance can be somewhat puzzling to a

50 *General view of Bodrum (ancient Halicarnassus) from the castle looking towards the site of the Mausoleum, below and to the right of the theatre on the hillside*

present-day visitor for the main structure of the tomb monument has completely disappeared. All that survives is a rectangular cutting in the rock for the foundations, the western staircase down which Maussollos' body was brought for burial, the reconstructed outlines of the tomb-chamber, and a litter of broken column drums and architectural stones (Figure 51).

There is virtually nothing left of the Mausoleum on its site. In order to attempt to reconstruct its original appearance we have to combine the evidence from a wide range of sources, much of it fragmentary or controversial in nature. This evidence falls into three main categories: first, information given by the ancient writers, notably the account of Pliny the Elder; second, surviving sculptural and architectural stones which were built into the Castle of St Peter at Bodrum by the Knights Hospitallers, who were responsible for dismantling the remains of the monument; and third, the finds from two major campaigns of excavation carried out on the site. The first of these was conducted by Sir Charles Newton between 1856 and 1858, as a result of which many large

51 *A view of the foundation-cutting for the Mausoleum from the west, showing the position of the tomb-chamber and the upturned blocking-stone*

fragments of sculpture and architecture are to be found today in the British Museum in London. The second is the recent Danish campaign led by Professor Kristian Jeppesen of Aarhus University between 1966 and 1977, which was responsible for the modern clearance and conservation of the site. We will look at each of these main sources in turn, before confronting the problem of the detailed reconstruction of the building.

By far the most important of the accounts in ancient writers is the partial description of the Mausoleum given by the Elder Pliny in his *Natural History* (XXXVI. 30–31), written about AD 75. This still remains fundamental to any reconstruction and is therefore given in translation from the Latin text of the Teubner edition:

> Scopas had as his rivals and contemporaries Bryaxis, Timotheus and Leochares, whom we must discuss together, because they jointly carved the sculptures of the Mausoleum. This is the tomb built by his wife Artemisia for Mausolus, king of Caria, who died in the second year of the 107th Olympiad. These artists in particular were responsible for

102

making the building one of the seven wonders of the world. It is 63 feet long on the north and south sides, shorter on the façades, its total circumference is 440 feet, it rises to a height of 25 cubits, and is surrounded by 36 columns. They called the circumference a 'colonnade'. The sculptures on the east side were carved by Scopas, those on the north by Bryaxis, those on the south by Timotheus, and those on the west by Leochares; and before they finished the queen died. But they did not stop the work until it was completed, considering it to be a monument to their own glory and artistic skill; and to this day their hands compete with one another. A fifth artist took part. For above the colonnade is a pyramid, equal in height to the lower part, contracting by 24 steps to the topmost point; on the summit is a marble four-horse chariot, made by Pythis. When this is included it brings the whole building to a height of 140 feet.

It can be seen that Pliny's account contains a number of detailed facts and figures which look as if they may derive from an authoritative source. But there are variant readings in the surviving manuscripts and some of the figures which are given do not seem to add up. For example, if the total circumference was 440 feet and there were longer sides at north and south (both of which points are supported by the evidence of the excavated foundations), then the length of each of those longer sides ought to have been much greater than the 63 feet cited in the text, at any rate at ground level. Making allowance for these difficulties, however, some sort of overall picture does emerge from the description and the following points are likely to be correct.

The Mausoleum was rectangular in plan, with sides at ground level probably of 120 and 100 feet, which add up to Pliny's circumference of 440 feeet. It was 140 feet high and consisted of three main parts: a lofty podium or base, called simply 'the lower part' in Pliny's account, perhaps 60 feet in height; above this a colonnade of 36 columns probably arranged 11 by 9 (eleven columns on each of the longer sides and nine on each of the shorter, counting the corner columns twice) – these columns we know from the excavations to have been of the Ionic order; and above this a roof in the form of a pyramid, with 24 steps reducing to a platform on which stood the crowning four-horse chariot. The 25 cubits, or 37½ feet, mentioned by Pliny, is evidently the height of one part of the building and in all probability refers to the height of the colonnade from column base to cornice. If so, then of the remaining amount of the overall height to be allotted, perhaps 22½ feet belonged to the pyramid roof and 20 feet to the chariot group and its base.

The other general point which can fairly be deduced from the text of Pliny, but which has not always been allowed for in past reconstructions, is that it was the lavishness and quality of the sculptured decoration of the Mausoleum which gave the building its repute. Pliny names four famous Greek sculptors who he says were responsible each for one side of the building: Scopas at the east, Bryaxis at the north, Timotheus at the south, and Leochares at the west. However, he mentions no individual sculptures except for the quadriga on the summit, which he says was by Pythis, who is usually thought to be the same person as the Pytheos named by Vitruvius (VII. *Praef.* 12–13) as one of the two authors of a book about the Mausoleum, the other being Satyros. Ultimately it may be this lost book by Pytheos and Satyros from which Pliny's account derives.

Among the many other brief references to the Mausoleum in ancient literature the short account by Vitruvius (*loc. cit.*) may be mentioned. Written about one hundred years earlier than Pliny's description, in *c.* 30–25 BC, it adds nothing of detail but includes the name of Praxiteles among the four sculptors, relegating Timotheos to a possible alternative. This is usually supposed to be an error.

So much then for the ancient sources. We turn now to Bodrum Castle, which has been both the cause of the destruction of the Mausoleum, and the means of preservation of some of its key elements.

It seems that the Mausoleum may have stood reasonably intact until the thirteenth century AD, at which date the upper part, including the roof and colonnade, probably fell down in an earthquake. There was, however, no wholesale destruction until the late fifteenth century. In 1494 the Knights of St John decided to refortify their castle at Bodrum (which had been built in 1402) and they used the remains of the Mausoleum as a convenient source of squared stone. Long stretches of walling in the castle are built from blocks of green volcanic stone which had formed the core of the Mausoleum. The blocks are generally about 90 cm square by 30 cm thick, and show clear traces of the clamps which once joined them together. The marble facing blocks of the

Mausoleum and its marble sculptures were mostly broken up into small pieces and burnt to make lime mortar. Recent research by Anthony Luttrell shows that this work of destruction went on for a period of 28 years until 1522, by which time almost every block had been removed from the Mausoleum down to the bottom of the foundations and the subterranean tomb-chamber had been opened up and looted.

A remarkable account of the destruction of the lower part of the Mausoleum and the discovery in 1522 of the then intact burial was published in French by Claude Guichard in 1581. Part of it reads as follows:

The Knights Hospitallers, on acquiring Bodrum, began to fortify the castle. And looking around for stone to make lime, and not finding any more suitable or more accessible than certain steps of white marble, raised in the form of a platform, in the middle of a field near the harbour where once the ancient forum had been, they knocked them down and took them away for this purpose. The stone being found to be good, they quickly used up what was above ground, and proceeded to dig down lower in the hope of finding more. In this they had great success, for they soon discovered that the deeper they dug the more the structure was enlarged at the base, providing them not only with stone for burning, but also for building.

After four or five days, having laid bare a large area, one afternoon they saw an opening like the entrance into a cave. Taking candles, they went down into it and found there a large square chamber surrounded by marble columns with their bases, capitals, architraves, friezes and cornices carved in relief. The space between the columns was lined with slabs and bands of marbles of different colours, ornamented with mouldings and sculptures which matched the rest of the work, and inserted in the white ground of the wall, where histories and battle scenes were also represented in relief. Having admired this at first, and entertained their fancy with the singularity of the work, finally they pulled it down, broke it apart and smashed it, in order to use it for the same purpose as the rest.

Beyond this chamber they found afterwards a very low doorway leading into another room like an antechamber, where there was a tomb with its urn and its gabled lid of white marble, very beautiful, and of marvellous lustre. This tomb, for lack of time they did not open, the retreat already having sounded. The next day, when they returned, they found the tomb opened and the earth all around strewn with fragments of gold cloth and spangles of the same metal, which made them think that the pirates, who hovered along this coast, having some inkling of what had been discovered, had visited the place during the night, and had removed the lid of the tomb. It is supposed that they discovered in it much treasure.

Unlikely though this story might sound, it has been confirmed at least in part by the finds of Jeppesen's recent excavations. In the vicinity of the tomb-chamber fragments of the gabled lid of the tomb were found, which seems in fact to have been a sarcophagus of white alabaster, while numerous small gold spangles, like those described by Guichard, in all probability belonged to the funeral cloth. From this it appears that the burial of Maussollos was much like that recently found intact at Vergina in Macedonia and ascribed to Philip II of Macedon (died 336 BC). The ashes and bones from the cremated body of Maussollos would have been wrapped in gold-embroidered cloth and placed perhaps in a gold larnax (box), which in turn would have been set within the sarcophagus of alabaster.

Whether there really was so elaborate a room above the tomb-chamber as is described by Guichard is much less certain. No traces of its rich decoration have been identified and it may be that architectural detail and sculptural decoration which was originally on the exterior of the tomb has inadvertently been transferred to the interior of this room in the retelling of the story.

Although tremendous damage was done to the Mausoleum by the Knights Hospitallers, they did not destroy quite all of the sculptured stones they found. Between 1505 and 1507 about a dozen slabs of the frieze showing the battle between Greeks and Amazons caught the eye of one of the commanders and were built into the walls of the castle for decoration, and so preserved. Among them was a single block from a second frieze with the battle of Lapiths and Centaurs. Also built into the castle at this time were the foreparts of four of the statues of standing lions and a running leopard from a hunting group. These sculptures were later taken to the British Museum, the friezes in 1846 and the lions and leopard in 1857.

The Castle walls continue to yield up their treasures. A complete architrave block reused as a lintel over a gateway has recently furnished the axial spacing of the columns, while a corner block of

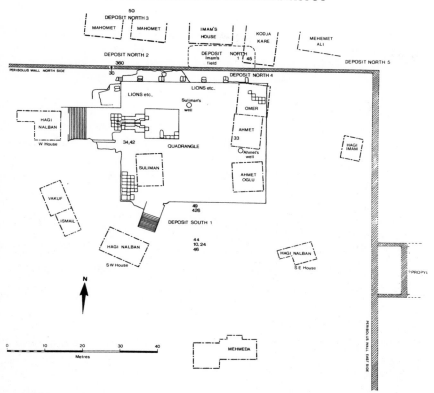

52 *Composite plan of the site of the Mausoleum combining discoveries from the excavations of Newton and Jeppesen*

the Amazon frieze, found in 1975 and not yet published, provides evidence that this ran round all four sides of the monument.

It was the relief sculptures and lions built into Bodrum Castle which led ultimately to Newton's excavations about 350 years after the Knights' destruction. Travellers who came this way in the late eighteenth and nineteenth centuries noticed the sculptures and guessed that they came from the Mausoleum. In 1846 Lord Stratford de Redcliffe, British Ambassador in Istanbul, managed to gain permission to remove the by now famous relief slabs of the Amazon frieze and bring them to London. Ten years later, in the hope of finding more such treasures, Charles T. Newton, then an assistant keeper at the British Museum, set out on a grand campaign to locate and excavate the site of the Mausoleum.

With the help of Vitruvius' description of Halicarnassus, and a certain amount of trial and error, Newton's team managed to locate the site of the Mausoleum. He purchased, not without some difficulty, the Turkish houses which then occupied the ground and, on New Year's Day 1857, proceeded to dig. His enthusiasm soon turned to disappointment as he discovered the extent of the Knights' devastation and realised that the Mausoleum had been almost entirely robbed. All that was left was the outline of the rectangular foundation area cut in the soft rock, with a few of the green-stone blocks from the core still in position. He called the whole area the Quadrangle (Figure 52) and recorded disconsolately in his later publication:

> the whole of the Quadrangle was filled with remains of architecture and sculpture. The quantity of these fragments was so great that it would have been impossible to specify their exact position on the Plan, nor would such information be of any value in reference to the majority of the marbles, which had evidently been rolled and pitched out of the way by the spoilers of the tomb, as they removed successive courses of masonry.

One of the larger fragments retrieved from this foundation area was a statue of a galloping horse ridden by a man wearing Persian dress, the whole group sculpted on a colossal scale, about one and two-thirds times life size (Figure 53). This statue, which may once have belonged to an extensive group representing a hunting scene or a battle, is of excellent design and most realistic execution, the oriental trousers over the right leg and the lower part of the tunic appearing to billow back in the wind as the rider speeds along. Sadly the original effect intended by the sculptor has been spoilt by the wanton damage inflicted, as the extremities of horse and rider were removed by blows of a sledge-hammer, no doubt to provide material for the lime-kilns.

In another part of the area of the Quadrangle Newton came upon a series of four adjoining slabs of the Amazon frieze, reused as covers over a later drain culvert (Figure 54). These show similar scenes of combat to the slabs recovered from the castle walls, but the detail of the figures which survive is much less weathered and the overall compositional design can be more readily appreciated with its varied forms and its powerful diagonal poses.

After spending three months carefully extracting hundreds of

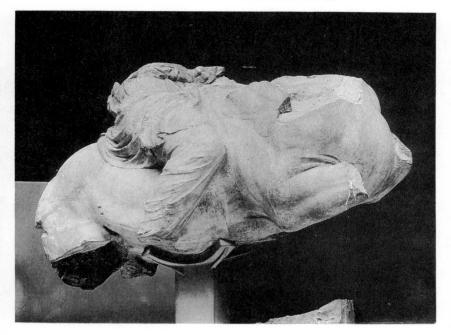

53 *Fragmentary statue of horse with Persian rider from the Quadrangle (foundation-cutting) of the Mausoleum. (British Museum)*

battered fragments from the ruin of the foundations, Newton turned his attention to the ground north of the building and immediately had better luck. Near the north-west corner of the building he came upon a well-preserved Ionic capital (Figure 55), together with an upper column drum. It is, in fact, a corner capital and is almost certainly that from the corner junction of the north and west colonnades of the Mausoleum. This was the first indication that the order employed on the Mausoleum was indeed Ionic. But it was the spectacular finds in the eastern half of the north side, in the field of a house belonging to the local Imam or priest, which were to change Newton's excavations almost overnight from comparative failure to spectacular success (Figure 52).

On the north side the ancient peribolos or precinct wall which surrounds the Mausoleum runs very close to the building, being only some 3.35m from its north face. Because the hill of the

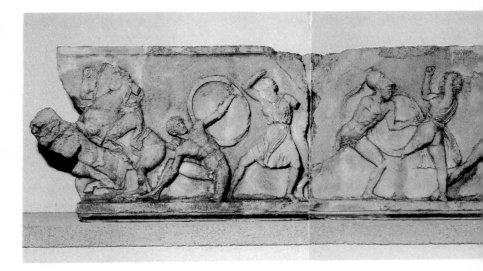

54 *Three adjoining slabs of the frieze showing the battle between Greeks and Amazons from the Quadrangle (foundation-cutting) of the Mausoleum. A sequence of twelve figures is preserved. (British Museum)*

Acropolis begins to rise up at this point there was also a deeper soil cover here. These two chance factors meant that sculptures and stones which fell to the north of the precinct wall were rapidly covered with earth and so were spared the ravages of the Knights of St John, who, as we have seen, destroyed the building working downwards from above.

So it was that in an area of ground in the Imam's field, measuring about 60 feet in length by 20 feet in width (20 by 6.5m), Newton came upon the only major undisturbed deposit of sculptures and architectural stones from the Mausoleum. An engraving based on a contemporary photograph, taken when the area had been cleared (Figure 56) includes a nice shot of the bearded Newton himself, leaning over the north peribolos wall in obvious satisfaction at having found something substantial at last. Architectural stones in the picture include blocks from the upper courses of the peribolos wall, steps from the pyramidal roof and fragments of architrave beams that once linked the columns. Even more important were the sculptures found. From this relatively small area came almost all the large sculptures to be seen in the

British Museum today. They include the splendid forehand and hindquarters of horses from the chariot group on the summit of the building (Figures 57 and 58); the colossal male and female portrait statues, clearly of members of the ruling dynasty of Halicarnassus, and understandably identified by Newton as Maussollos and Artemisia, although there is no proof that this is so (Figure 59); several lion statues like those from the Castle walls, but better preserved (Figure 60); and a fine head of the god Apollo, the only deity known to have been represented amongst the free-standing sculptures of the Mausoleum. Altogether 66 statues or fragments of statues were found in this one deposit. They belonged to at least twenty different statues of varying subject-matter and scales, although all were over life size. It was quite a haul, and the truest indication of how lavish the sculptured decoration of the Mausoleum once was.

The deposit has an added significance for a reconstruction of the building from its proximity to the peribolos wall. It is a reasonable supposition that the sculptures found in the deposit must have been set high enough up on the structure to have fallen

111

55 *Ionic corner capital and upper column drum, probably from the north-west angle column of the Mausoleum. (British Museum)*

or been thrown beyond the peribolos wall when the building collapsed. The higher a sculpture was placed, the greater the chance of finishing up here. This interpretation is supported by the contents of the deposit. The sculptures which we *know* to have been highest placed are best represented here: the chariot horses and the lions (of which there are 3 statues and 19 fragments). The largest of the three scales of human statuary is also well represented in the colossal statues of 'Maussollos' and 'Artemisia' and several fragments of similar figures. Of the intermediate scale of figures, however, there are only fragments of heads and bodies, but no feet; while of the life-size scale of statues, known to have existed from fragments found elsewhere on the site, there is no certain example. It is for this reason I have suggested that the life-size sculptures were placed lowest on the Mausoleum, and low enough to ensure that none could span the peribolos wall, which was still two metres high when Newton excavated. The positions of the other sculptures may have been graded upwards according to scale, culminating in the chariot group on the summit of the building, which was twice life-size. The Imam's field deposit,

56 *A view of the deposit of architectural stones and sculptures found in the Imam's field on the north side of the Mausoleum. (After an engraving in Newton's* History of Discoveries, *pl. XI, above.)*

containing as it does sculptures from less than half of one side of the building, constitutes an important vertical control on any reconstruction of the sculptural decoration.

Newton also brought back to England as many of the architectural stones as he could manage, and they are now laid out in rows in a British Museum storeroom in west London. These stones, which contain vital evidence for a reconstruction of the building, are still being studied and await their definitive publication. Among them are many steps from the pyramid roof, including an almost complete corner step which proves that the treads of the steps on the longer and shorter sides of the building were of different widths: the wider tread of 54 cm probably belonged to the shorter sides (the west and east), while the narrower tread of 43 cm would be that of the longer north and south sides.

57 *Forehand of chariot horse with original bronze bridle attached, from the group on the summit of the Mausoleum. (British Museum)*

With the aid of these dimensions, combined with the numbers of pyramid steps (24) and columns (36) given by Pliny, Newton and his architect Pullan managed to produce a reasonable reconstruction of the roof and upper part of the Mausoleum, but they failed satisfactorily to accommodate the many different groups and scales of sculptures, in the round and in relief, to the building. One of their main difficulties was the lack of an accurate and detailed plan of the foundation-cutting, and therefore of the lower dimensions of the building. Newton's team of Royal Engineers tended to employ the cut-and-fill or mining techniques of the Victorian railway navigator, with the result that the whole of the Quadrangle had never been laid bare at any one time. In any case, most of this work had been completed and filled in again before Pullan even arrived on the site. This serious deficiency was not remedied until the new excavations carried out by Kristian Jeppesen between 1966 and 1977.

If the discovery of the deposit of sculptures in the Imam's field

58 *Reconstructed profile view of chariot group with surviving fragments drawn in outline*

was the highlight of Newton's excavation, the greatest achievement of Jeppesen's has been the clearing and accurate planning of the foundation-cutting, and the retrieval of architectural and sculptural fragments left within it. The composite plan (Figure 52) shows the main features within the foundation area and the relationship of the cutting itself to the north and east walls of the peribolos and the propylon, or entrance gateway, a few remains of which have been discovered in the centre of the east wall. Dotted lines indicate houses which occupied the site before Newton's excavation and which were purchased and demolished by him. A huge conical spoil heap left over the Quadrangle by Newton effectively prevented the reconstruction of houses on the site after his departure, although a new house was built over the site of the deposit in the Imam's field.

It can be seen that the tomb-chamber does not occupy a central place in the plan of the building but is towards the north-west corner of it. Possibly this may have been to delude would-be tomb robbers, more likely it may have been placed there to

59 *Colossal statues of male and female Carian rulers, often identified as Maussollos and Artemisia, from the deposit in the Imam's field on the north side of the Mausoleum. (British Museum)*

associate it with an earlier tomb on the site, perhaps that of Artemisia I of Halicarnassus, who fought on the side of the Persian King Xerxes against the Greeks at the battle of Salamis in 480 BC. In this way Maussollos would emphasise a dynastic link which in terms of blood-ties was probably not strong at all. Important tombs certainly existed on this site prior to the Mausoleum, as is shown by the staircase near the south-west corner, which was cut through by the Mausoleum foundations.

The broad staircase cut into the rock on the western side of the Quadrangle leads down to the entrance to the tomb-chamber and

116

60 *Best-preserved lion statue, from the Imam's field deposit.*
(British Museum)

was evidently made for Maussollos' funeral. The huge green stone which blocked the entrance to the tomb still survives (Figure 51). It was in its original position when Newton dug, but his men tipped it over, revealing on the underside an intricate system of cuttings and dowels intended to drop into place when the stone was pushed in. Cuttings on the front and top of the stone indicate the vain attempts of later tomb robbers to force an entry. In front of this stone at the foot of the staircase was a great heap of stones which Newton took to be a disintegrated wall. When removed by Jeppesen, however, it turned out that the stones were not a wall at all but were a protective weight on top of a ritual deposit of food, made presumably immediately after the entombment of Maussollos' remains. This offering of food consisted of some whole carcases of sheep, other carefully butchered cuts of sheep or goat, calf and ox, some chickens, doves, a goose, and a considerable quantity of eggs. Such a food offering for the spirit of the departed conforms to Near Eastern rather than Greek funerary practice.

Some of the most important architectural features of the foundations are the green volcanic blocks like those from the castle still in place in the south-west and north-east corners. These show that the foundations for the podium of the Mausoleum almost completely filled the cutting, and they provide maximum dimensions for the base of the building of 38 metres for the longer sides and 32 metres for the shorter. This is in reasonable agreement with Pliny's figure for the circumference of the building of 440 feet, if the Greek foot length employed was 32cm, as is possible. On this basis the dimensions 38.40m and 32m would give side lengths of 120 and 100 feet.

Further evidence for the reconstruction of the building has come from architectural stones found within the foundation area by Jeppesen. Several fragments of wider pyramid steps with cuttings for statues prove that the lion-statues were placed at the base of the roof. Fragments of statue bases in blue limestone with moulded front edges and cuttings for statues evidently came from the podium, and prove that free-standing sculptures were accommodated on ledges against the wall of the podium, probably on more than one level. There are about twenty of these stones surviving, mostly for life-size sculptures in action. One stone in particular is important because it provides the full projection of the step. This is only 72cm, quite shallow, showing that the statues on it were set very close to the wall like pedimental sculptures. Facing-blocks in blue limestone further suggest that certain parts of the podium were finished in this darker stone to contrast with the white marble of the rest of the architecture and the polychrome of the sculptures.

Two other crucial discoveries have been made by Jeppesen in the course of his excavations. One, already mentioned briefly, is the calculation of the axial spacing of the columns of the order, which is worked out from the complete architrave beam found in the Castle and which turns out to be almost exactly 3 metres. If we suppose with Pliny that there were 36 columns, and that they were arranged 11 by 9, this would give maximum dimensions for the top of the podium of 32m on the longer sides and 26m on the shorter, indicating the amount by which the podium was stepped inwards, about 3m on each side. A stepped podium is in agreement with the remark by Guichard that the deeper the Knights dug 'the more the structure was enlarged at its base'. The other is the discovery of the sequence of stones which effected the

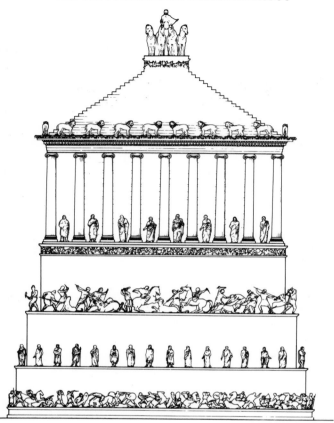

61 *Suggested reconstruction of one of the shorter sides of the Mausoleum. (After Waywell)*

transition from the podium to the peristyle, and the virtual proof that the Amazon frieze was positioned at the top of the podium, immediately below the colonnade. If so, it would originally have been some 116m in length, of which about one quarter is well-preserved.

A provisional reconstruction of one of the shorter sides of the Mausoleum, based on that first published ten years ago, illustrates a likely arrangement of the varied sculptures on the building (Figure 61). It incorporates the evidence from the different sources already discussed above. The numbers of pyramid steps and columns are taken from Pliny. So too is the overall height of 140

119

feet (44.80m on the basis of a 32cm foot), of which 60 feet is allotted to the podium, 37½ feet to the colonnade, 22½ feet to the pyramid, and 20 feet to the chariot group and its base. Known dimensions which fit this scheme include the following: the height and tread of the pyramid steps (height 30cm; tread 60cm for the lowest step, otherwise 43cm for the longer sides, and 54cm for the shorter), the axial spacing of the columns (3m), the width of the base of the monument (32m on this shorter side), the projection of the lowest step of the podium (72cm), and the sizes of statues and friezes. Sculptures whose positions are fixed are the chariot group on the summit, the lions at the base of the roof, the Amazon frieze at the top of the podium and the life-size fighting figures at its base. Also within the peristyle the ceiling coffers were decorated with cover slabs carved in relief with the exploits of Theseus. The positions of the other sculptures are negotiable, as it were, but if we accept that all the statues and friezes were externally placed there is only limited room for manoeuvre.

We know for sure that there was no frieze in the Ionic entablature of the order and so, of the two unplaced friezes which survive, that with the fight between Lapiths and Centaurs may plausibly be attributed to the base of the chariot group, while the chariot race could have been inserted into the upper part of the wall behind the colonnade. In this way a sculptured frieze would have decorated the top of each of the three main architectural parts of the Mausoleum.

Most important among the unplaced sculptures in the round are the colossal portrait statues, of which the so-called Maussollos and Artemisia are the best preserved of an extensive series that seems to have represented the ruling dynasty of Caria and their ancestors. These are most reasonably placed in prime position between the columns of the peristyle, although it must be stressed that there is no proof that they stood here nor, if they did, whether they rested on bases.

The other free-standing sculptures belong in the main to groups of lateral design that were evidently set on narrow bases against the wall of the podium in the manner of pedimental sculptures. The number of steps and their height above ground level is not known for certain, and this remains the most schematic part of the reconstruction. As the sculptures are of three different scales, ranging from life-size up to one and two-thirds times life-size, the writer has suggested that there ought to have been three separate ledges to accommodate them, for which sufficient room is available in the stepping out of the podium between its top and base. Jeppesen, however, at present favours two rather than three steps to the podium and would set them rather closer together than in this reconstruction. Subjects represented include colossal-scale animal hunts and scenes of offering or sacrifice, and a life-size battle between Greek and Persian warriors, some of whom were mounted on horseback. There are also numerous quiet standing figures, probably portraits, some male, some female, who are of intermediate (so-called heroic) scale, and here are placed on an intermediate level between the two action groups. The sculptures from the podium suffered most severely at the hands of the Knights and now survive only in small fragments, although those fragments are very numerous. In the reconstruction the heights of the steps on the podium are divided in the proportion 3:4:5 to suit the scale of the sculptures associated with them.

Quite apart from the problems of the podium, there are many other difficulties which remain. Who stood in the chariot and what was its meaning, set high on the building? The stocky proportions of the horses and the large-wheeled chariot suggest a satrapal, ceremonial character. There must have been an occupant and, if so, he must have represented Maussollos in one guise or another. But was he shown as man or god, or was it deliberately left ambiguous? There is no historical evidence that Maussollos regarded himself as a god, but to a Greek mind such an elevated position for the chariot group would surely have implied deification.

Were the lions from the roof arranged in pairs or in facing lines? The latter is favoured because some of the lions have more sharply turned heads, which could be the leading animals of each line, but there is really no strong evidence one way or the other. On the later Heroon at Belevi, near Ephesos, the similarly-placed griffins were definitely arranged in pairs, but with a vase in between for which there is no evidence on the Mausoleum.

What of the interior of the building? Again there is minimal evidence but, judging from the quantities of green volcanic stone from the core reused in the castle, much of it must have been solid. Jeppesen has suggested that there were two internal rooms with corbelled roofs, as occurs in some Egyptian pyramids, one above the tomb-chamber, and one taking the place of the conventional Greek 'cella', behind the colonnade. Was there a way into the structure? It would be surprising if there were not, if only for maintenance purposes, but again we simply do not know.

What then are we to make of this curious, expensive, apparently useless structure? Was it merely the random product of the megalomaniac ambition of Maussollos (or Artemisia), or did it embody a subtler symbolism? There is little doubt that the basic reason for its existence was as a founder's tomb, celebrating Maussollos as founder, or more correctly, refounder of Halicarnassus. It was not intended to be a dynastic tomb to receive all the royal burials of the ruling house of Caria, nor is there any reason to suppose that anyone other than Maussollos was ever buried in it. But the size of the monument and the lavishness of its finish do suggest ulterior motives.

It is arguable that the strange architectural form results from an attempt to combine features from three different civilisations, Lycian, Greek and Egyptian. The high, rectangular podium is characteristic of Lycian tomb architecture, a well-known example being the Nereid Monument from Xanthos, now partly reconstructed in the British Museum. Above this the peristyle is Ionic Greek of the Ephesian variety, with plinths and elaborate bases supporting slender fluted columns, trim volute capitals and a relatively low entablature enriched with dentils and mouldings. The ingenious stepped or pyramidal roof is probably Egyptianising, although some would see it merely as an ornate elevated base for the chariot group. The overall dressing of this hybrid structure in Greek architectural and sculptural forms produced by the best Greek artists of the day attests Maussollos' predilection for Greek culture, but the monument as a whole could be seen as a statement of Carian supremacy over all these contributory civilisations. Possibly, therefore, the Mausoleum was intended to symbolise the fusion of Greek and non-Greek civilisations which Maussollos and Artemisia hoped would result from the establishment of a Carian empire with Halicarnassus as its capital. It did not turn out that way, but a generation later Alexander of Macedon was to achieve what was very probably Maussollos' dream.

Lucian, writing in the second century AD, was more down-to-earth and cynical in his interpretation. In his *Dialogues of the Dead* he stages an imaginary confrontation in the underworld between Diogenes, the Cynic philosopher, and Maussollos, and the prophetic words may serve as a suitable epitaph for the Mausoleum itself.

'Tell me Carian', says Diogenes, 'why are you so proud and why do you expect to be honoured more than the rest of us?'

'Because', replies Maussollos, 'I was handsome and tall and victorious in war. But most of all, because I have lying over me in Halicarnassus a gigantic monument such as no other dead person has, adorned in the finest way with statues of horses and men carved most realistically from the best quality marble'.

Diogenes answers: 'My handsome Maussollos, your strength and beauty are no longer with you here. If we were to have a beauty contest, I can't see why your skull should be thought better than mine. And as for your tomb and that expensive marble, it may give the people of Halicarnassus something to show off and boast about to tourists, but I can't see what benefit you get from it, unless you're claiming that you have a heavier burden to bear than the rest of us, being weighed down by so much stone'.

'Is all this nothing then?' exclaims Maussollos. 'Are Maussollos and Diogenes equal?'

'No your highness', replies Diogenes, 'we are not equal. Maussollos will groan when he remembers things on earth which he thought brought him happiness, while Diogenes will laugh at him. Maussollos will talk of the tomb built for him at Halicarnassus by his wife Artemisia, while Diogenes does not even know if his body has a tomb. Nor does he care. He has left to future generations an account that he has lived the life of a good man, an account that is loftier than your memorial, most servile of Carians, and built on surer foundations'.

THE COLOSSUS
OF RHODES

REYNOLD HIGGINS

THE ISLAND of Rhodes is situated off the south-west corner of Asia Minor at the junction of two ancient sea-lanes, one running between Miletus on the Ionian coast and the cities of Egypt and Cyrenaica, the other between Greece and the cities of Cyprus and Syria. This favourable geographical position, coupled with the fertile soil and excellent climate, ensured a degree of prosperity for the island. For long it was divided into three territories, ruled from the cities of Ialysos on the north, Lindos on the east and Kamiros on the west.

In 408 BC, for reasons which are unclear but which may have been commercial, the three city-states combined and built for themselves a federal capital on the north tip of the island, to which they gave the name Rhodes. It was an ideal situation, which they exploited by the creation of no less than five harbours.

The new city grew rapidly and soon boasted between 60,000 and 80,000 inhabitants. Covering about the same area as the modern city, it was laid out on the grid-iron plan made famous by Hippodamus of Miletus. Very little indeed can be seen of this plan today as medieval and modern Rhodes overlies the ancient city (Figure 62); but much of it has in fact been recovered in recent years by means of rescue excavations and aerial photography (Figure 63).

In 377 BC Rhodes joined the second Island Confederacy formed by Athens (the first had been in 477), but she withdrew in 356 at the instigation of Maussollos of Caria, who set up a garrison there. Because Rhodes had sided with the Persians when Alexander the Great was besieging Tyre, she received a Macedonian garrison after the fall of Tyre in 332 BC. When it later became evident that Alexander the Great was the man of the moment, Rhodes wisely took his part and so escaped disaster.

On Alexander's death in 323 BC his generals quarrelled amongst themselves for the succession and eventually divided up his empire between them. Rhodes at first preserved a precarious independence, but it was too good to last. She sided with Ptolemy of Egypt for commercial reasons against Antigonus, like Ptolemy, one of Alexander's generals. Antigonus, the One-Eyed, had been governor of Phrygia and was later to be king of Macedonia, founder of the Antigonid dynasty. After Alexander's death he held the strongest power in Asia, commander-in-chief of the Grand Army of 60,000 men and possessor of Alexander's treasure chest of over 25,000 talents of gold. The Antigonids were constantly harassing Ptolemy I of Egypt in the Mediterranean; they had defeated his brother Menelaus at Salamis in Cyprus and then Ptolemy himself when he sailed to the rescue in 306. Then Antigonus attacked Ptolemy on his own Egyptian frontier at Pelusium, but was forced to withdraw.

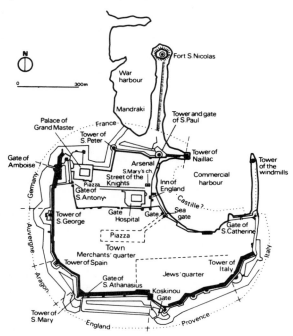

62 *Plan of Rhodes in the Middle Ages. (After A.R. Burn)*

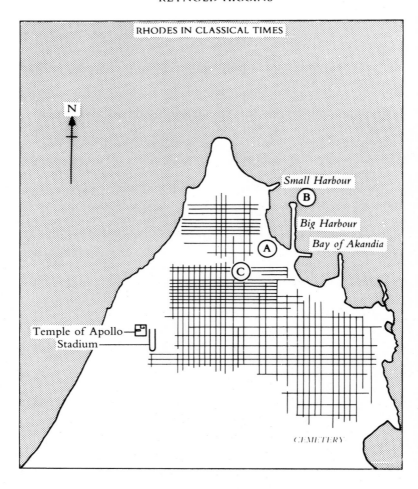

RHODES IN CLASSICAL TIMES

N

Small Harbour

B

Big Harbour

Bay of Akandia

A

C

Temple of Apollo
Stadium

CEMETERY

63 *Plan of excavated streets and sites in Rhodes. A The deigma (bazaar);
B Later Fort St Nicolas; C Temple of Helios (?) (After C. Karousos)*

In 307 BC Antigonus called upon the Rhodians to join him in a war against Ptolemy but, as they enjoyed a prosperous trading relationship with Egypt, they refused. The result of this refusal was the famous siege of Rhodes in 305 BC, undertaken by Demetrius, son of Antigonus, known as Poliorcetes ('the Besieger'). This became famous as the success of the free city

126

against the tyranny of monarchy – of a David against Goliath. Demetrius arrived with 40,000 soldiers, 30,000 workmen, 200 warships and 170 transport ships. His siege engines included a huge armoured tower, full of catapults and slingers, called Helepolis ('the Taker of Cities'). But, for once, the Besieger had met his match. After a year he was compelled to raise the siege, in spite of having employed the latest and most sophisticated equipment. Antigonus ordered his son to make terms – they were what the Rhodians had wanted in the first instance: to be free and to be Antigonus' ally against all except Ptolemy of Egypt.

Demetrius was so impressed with the bravery of the Rhodian people (even their slaves had served on the walls during the siege), that he left behind him all his siege engines. The great balls of stone hurled by the catapults remain to this day. The Rhodians sold the equipment for a large sum of money which they spent on the creation and erection of an enormous bronze statue of their patron deity, Helios the Sun God. The sculptor they chose for the commission was Chares of Lindos, a pupil of the famous sculptor Lysippus. Between 294 and 282 BC Chares and his bronze-casters set to work to produce a statue 70 cubits high (about 33m, 110ft).

We know less about the Colossus than about any other of the Seven Wonders. We do not know where it stood or what it looked like; but scholars have found it possible and not entirely unprofitable to assemble all the available evidence and to make a number of guesses on both counts.

First, the meaning of the word Colossus. It was originally a pre-Greek, Western Asiatic word for a statue or statuette. In that sense it was taken over by the Dorian Greeks when they settled in the Dodecanese and south-west Asia Minor about 1000 BC, and so it was originally applied to Chares' statue of Helios. After the creation of that statue, however, and its inclusion amongst the Seven Wonders of the Ancient World, the word came to be restricted to gigantic statues.

Although the Colossus of Rhodes is mentioned some sixteen times by ancient writers, only three have much to say, and their accounts raise more questions than they answer. These writers are Strabo, Pliny the Elder and Philo of Byzantium. A fourth source is a Greek poem which is believed to be the dedicatory inscription of the statue.

In more recent times, many people have written about the Colossus from the fifteenth century onwards. Their views have been admirably summarised by the French scholar, A. Gabriel, in an article published in 1932; he also contributed a number of fruitful ideas of his own. Very little work of any consequence has been done on this subject since Gabriel's article. An article by Herbert Maryon, published in 1954, produced many novel suggestions, especially on the technical side. They were, however, for the most part rapidly demolished by Denys Haynes; but they did inspire him to publish the first credible account of how the Colossus was actually made.

We know all too little about the appearance of the statue, but references to it by Pliny and Strabo are worth quoting, incomplete though they are. Pliny wrote (*Natural History*, XXXIV, 41):

> Calling for admiration before all others was the colossal Statue of the Sun at Rhodes made by Chares of Lindos, pupil of Lysippus mentioned above. This statue was 70 cubits [33m or about 110ft] high; and, 56 years after its erection, was overthrown by an earthquake, but even lying on the ground it is a marvel. Few people can make their arms meet round the thumb of the figure, and the fingers are larger than most statues; and where the limbs have broken off enormous cavities yawn, while inside are seen great masses of rock with the weight of which the artist steadied it when he erected it. It is recorded that it took twelve years to complete and cost 300 talents [about £1.5 million], money realised from the engines of war belonging to King Demetrius which he had abandoned when he got tired of the protracted siege of Rhodes.

Strabo's account in his *Geography* (XIV, 2.5) runs:

> The city of the Rhodians lies on the eastern promontory of Rhodes; and it is so far superior to all others in harbours and roads and walls and improvements in general that I am unable to speak of any other city as equal to it, or even as almost equal to it, much less superior to it. It is remarkable also for its good order, and for its careful attention to the administration of affairs of state in general; and in particular to that of naval affairs, whereby it held the mastery of the sea for a long time and overthrew the business of piracy, and became a friend to the Romans and to all kings who favoured both the Romans and the Greeks.
>
> Consequently it not only has remained autonomous but also has been adorned with many votive offerings, which for the most part are to be found in the Dionysium and the

64 *Possible reconstruction of the Colossus standing with legs together and holding aloft a torch*

gymnasium, but partly in other places. The best of these are, first, the Colossus of Helius . . . 'seven times ten cubits in height, the work of Chares the Lindian'; but it now lies on the ground, having been thrown down by an earthquake and broken at the knees. In accordance with a certain oracle, the people did not raise it again. This, then, is the most excellent of the votive offerings (at any rate, it is by common agreement one of the Seven Wonders).

These accounts tell us very little as to what the Colossus looked like but common sense, coupled with what the ancient writers say, and also what they do not say, leads to the conclusion that the god was portrayed standing upright and probably naked.

We may go further and suggest that, to remain upright, a 33-metre statue would have to be very simple, approximately columnar in shape and in attitude not unlike an archaic Greek *kouros* figure. At the outset, Maryon's reconstruction, showing a naked man raising his right hand to his head, must be rejected. It is based on a fragmentary marble relief found on Rhodes which quite clearly portrays an athlete crowning himself and has nothing to do with Helios. On the basis of all the available evidence, Gabriel has produced a possible, but by no means certain, reconstruction, which consists of a naked young man standing stiffly erect, with legs together holding a torch in one hand and a spear in the other (Figure 64).

For the god's head, scholars have always turned to representations of the head of Helios on contemporary Rhodian coins. Most coins of around this date have a head surmounted by the sun's rays, and this was indeed a popular way of portraying Helios. But another variety of head, without rays, also occurs on contemporary Rhodian coins, so the question must be regarded as open, with a certain bias in favour of the rayed head (Figure 65).

The most surprising thing about the statue is its enormous size and this must have been as impressive in its fallen state as when it stood erect. Most accounts agree on a height of 70 cubits. One source, which gives 80 cubits, could well have included the base. The cubit varied somewhat in antiquity from time to time and place to place, but we would surely be right in giving the Colossus a height of about 33 metres or 110 feet.

Statues of up to 10 metres (30ft), were not unknown in ancient Greece, but nothing so large as the Colossus is recorded in antiquity before or after its creation. Possibly the inspiration came from Egypt, where enormous stone statues were known from an early date, and we know that Rhodes and Egypt were closely connected in the third century BC. One of the very few statues in modern times on this scale is the bronze Statue of Liberty on Bedloe's Island in New York Harbour (Figure 66). It was made by the French sculptor Auguste Bartholdi, with the Colossus of Rhodes in mind. Dedicated in 1886 to commemorate the French and American revolutions, it is 46 metres (152 feet) high; even taller than the Colossus.

To understand the incredibly complicated method by which the Colossus was constructed, we cannot do better than refer to the account of Philo of Byzantium, as translated and interpreted by Denys Haynes. As he points out, there is no doubt whatsoever that it was cast in sections and that Herbert Maryon was mistaken in proposing that it was made of hammered bronze plates. Philo says:

At Rhodes was set up a Colossus of seventy cubits high, representing the Sun; for the appearance of the God was

65 Obverses of silver tetradrachms (4-drachma pieces) of Rhodes with the head of Helios shown radiate and non-radiate. (British Museum)

known only to his descendants. The artist expended as much bronze on it as seemed likely to create a dearth in the mines: for the casting of the statue was an operation in which the bronze industry of the whole world was concerned. . . .

The artist fortified the bronze from within by means of an iron framework and squared blocks of stone, whose tie-bars bear witness to hammering of Cyclopean force. Indeed, the hidden part of the labour is greater than the visible. . . .

Having built a base of white marble, the artist first fixed upon it the feet of the Colossus up to the height of the ankle-joints, having worked out the proportions suitable to a divine image destined to stand to a height of seventy cubits; for the sole of the foot already exceeded in length the height of other statues. For this reason it was impossible to hoist up the rest of the statue and place it upon the feet, but the ankles had to be cast upon the feet and, as when a house is built, the whole work had to rise upon itself.

And for this reason, while other statues are first modelled, then dismembered for casting in parts, and finally recomposed and erected, in this case, after the first part had been cast, the second was modelled upon it, and for the following part again the same method of working was adopted. For the individual metal sections could not be moved.

After the casting of the new course upon that part of the work already completed, the spacing of the horizontal tie-

131

66 *The Statue of Liberty in New York Harbour*

bars and the joints of the framework were looked to, and the stability of the stone blocks placed within the figure was ensured. In order to prosecute the plan of operations on a firm basis throughout, the artist heaped up a huge mound of earth round each section as soon as it was completed, thus burying the finished work under the accumulated earth, and carrying out the casting of the next part on the level.

So, going up bit by bit, he reached the goal of his endeavour, and at the expense of 500 talents of bronze and 300 of iron, he created, with incredible boldness, a god similar to the real God; for he gave a second Sun to the world.

It is clear that with such a method of construction the figure would probably not have had arms outstretched in any way except perhaps upwards. The fact that Chares was the pupil of Lysippus also tells us something of the look that was in fashion at the time the statue was made. Although not in motion, the statue could not have had the austere and heavy immobility of archaic Greek *kouroi*. Lysippus rejoiced in achieving a supple feeling of movement in a relaxed athletic body and the Helios of Chares must have been in this tradition.

The situation of the Colossus is not recorded in any ancient source, an omission which has given rise to a number of attempts to locate it, all of which have been analysed by Gabriel.

We may disregard the theory that the statue was situated in the *deigma*, or bazaar, to the south-east of Mandraki Harbour, as it is based on a mis-reading of certain ancient texts. It has also been stated that there was a medieval chapel in the lower town, dedicated to St John of the Colossus, which had been erected on the site of the Colossus. Gabriel has shown that no such chapel existed in that part of the town.

The belief that the statue bestrode the harbour later known as Mandraki is first mentioned by an Italian pilgrim by the name of de Martoni, who visited Rhodes in 1394 and 1395. He quotes a

67 *Sixteenth-century engraving by Maerten van Heemskerck showing the Colossus bestriding the harbour entrance*

popular tradition that the statue had one foot where the church of
St Nicolas stood in his day (that is where Fort St Nicolas stands
today), at the eastern entrance to Mandraki Harbour, while the
other foot rested at the other side of the harbour entrance. This is,
of course, quite impossible as the span of the statue's legs would
have been, as Gabriel pointed out, over 400 metres (about 1300
feet). Yet this story, coupled with the view that the Colossus held
a torch to serve as a lighthouse, had a wide currency in the Middle
Ages, both in written accounts and in a number of drawings
(Figure 67). Indeed, it must have been one of these drawings that
Shakespeare had in mind when he made Cassius say of Julius
Caesar:

> Why, man, he doth bestride the narrow world
> Like a Colossus; and we petty men
> Walk under his huge legs, and peep about . . .
>
> *(Julius Caesar*, Act 1, 2, 134–7)

This belief may well have been inspired by a misunderstanding of
a poem preserved in the Greek Anthology which was, in all
probability, the dedicatory inscription of the Colossus:

> To you, oh Sun, the people of Dorian Rhodes set up this
> bronze statue reaching to Olympus, when they had pacified
> the waves of war and crowned their city with the spoils taken
> from the enemy. Not only over the seas but also on land did
> they kindle the lovely torch of freedom and independence.
> For to the descendants of Herakles belongs dominion over sea
> and land.

Inspired, possibly, by the previous belief is one which goes back
to the fifteenth century, that the Colossus stood where de Martoni
placed its right foot, at the eastern entrance to Mandraki Harbour
(Figure 68). Here, in the time of the Knights, was first a church,
then a fort (which still survives), dedicated to St Nicolas. This is
the situation which Gabriel prefers and it has much to recommend
it. There is undoubtedly much ancient masonry incorporated in
the fort and Gabriel has demonstrated that it would just have been
possible for the ruins not to have fallen into the sea but to have
rested on the land, a situation for which there is good authority.
We also know that after the building of the Colossus it became
customary to set colossal statues at the entrances of harbours, such
statues being recorded from Ostia the port of Rome and Caesarea

68 *View of the entrance to the Mandraki Harbour. Deer (one of the emblems of modern Rhodes) stand on the top of tall pillars which flank the actual harbour entrance. On the far side is Fort St Nicolas*

in Palestine. The latter is mentioned by Josephus in his *Jewish War*: 'The harbour mouth faced north, and on either side rose three colossal statues standing on pillars.' The harbour had been built by Herod the Great in 22–20 BC. Depictions of similar statues appear on coins as an essential element in the representations of a harbour. Several of these, which acted as beacons at the mouths of harbours, must have been of gigantic size. Most, like the Statue of Liberty, stood on a tall base. In particular those at Patras and Mothone in the Peloponnese, Caesarea Germanica in Bithynia and Soli-Pompeiopolis in Cilicia show how in Roman times the practice of erecting large statues on harbour moles was common-place.

There are, however, two principal objections to this theory that the statue stood at the mouth of the harbour. In the first place, it seems unlikely that the Rhodians would have allowed such an important and valuable piece of land to be occupied indefinitely

69 *The Turkish school at the head of the Street of Knights*

by the ruins of the statue after its destruction in 226 BC. Second, one ancient author tells us that in its fall the Colossus knocked down many houses. On a harbour wall this could not have happened.

This leads us to a final suggestion, which seems to the writer the most likely. At the top of the Street of Knights is an old Turkish school (Figure 69). It is known to have been built in the nineteenth century on the site of the conventual church of the Knights, dedicated to St John of the Colossus. This church, begun in 1310, was accidentally blown up by a gunpowder explosion in 1856. Before we make too much of the title 'St John of the Colossus', it should be pointed out that, thanks to the fame of this statue, the adjective *colossensis* ('of the Colossus') was applied in the Middle Ages to the entire city of Rhodes.

Nevertheless, from a number of inscriptions found near this spot, it is virtually certain that the Temple of Helios stood here or hereabouts in antiquity. It was usual practice amongst the Greeks to dedicate thank offerings in the sanctuaries of their gods, so that the great sanctuaries such as Delphi and Olympia became treasure houses of sculpture. Since we know that the Colossus was a thank offering for delivery from the siege of Demetrius, it is in the sanctuary of Helios that it would naturally be erected. If the St Nicolas site is to be ruled out, this area has a great deal to be said for it and could well repay excavation. At present there is certainly ancient masonry to be seen around the base of the school building, perhaps indicating that it is set four-square on the ancient foundations. Also, remains of ancient walls can be seen immediately outside the school gates and in the lower courses of the school perimeter wall that faces the Palace of the Grand Masters.

The earthquake which toppled the Colossus (and much of the city of Rhodes besides) occurred about 226 BC. Strabo records that the statue broke at the knees (Figure 70). Ptolemy III of Egypt immediately offered to pay for the restoration of the Colossus, but his offer was declined as the Rhodians had been forbidden by an oracle to re-erect it. So it lay where it fell for nearly 900 years and passers-by could look inside the ruins and see the mass of stone and iron which had once held it up.

When the Arabs plundered Rhodes in AD 654 they transported the fragments of the Colossus across the strait to Asia Minor and sold them to a Jew from Emesa. Tradition has it that he removed them to Syria on the backs of 900 camels. So ends the story of the Colossus of Rhodes, the least known of the Seven Wonders.

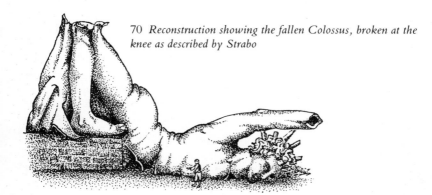

70 *Reconstruction showing the fallen Colossus, broken at the knee as described by Strabo*

137

THE PHAROS AT
ALEXANDRIA

PETER A. CLAYTON

THE PHAROS, the great lighthouse of Alexandria on the north-west coast of the Egyptian Delta, was the latest building to be added to what became the accepted canon of the Seven Wonders of the Ancient World. It took its name from the island in front of the harbour of Alexandria upon which it was built and, subsequently, gave that name as a generic term to later lighthouses.

The island of Pharos is a limestone outcrop that gave a good base in the midst of the surrounding sand and alluvial wash from the River Nile. Homer was the first to mention Pharos as an island in the *Odyssey*, and he locates it a day's sail from Egypt (also repeated later by Pliny). Obviously his sources were somewhat unsound. Legend told of the beautiful Helen coming to Egypt with Paris, but she was bored with the island since there was nothing to see and its only inhabitants were seals. She made another visit ten years later, but this time in the company of her husband Menelaus, returning home from Troy and blown off course to land there. Menelaus, the story goes, found an old man and asked him, 'What island is this?' The old man replied that it was Pharaoh's. Menelaus misheard and requestioned, 'Pharos?' to which the old man replied in the affirmative, repeating the word pharaoh in the old Egyptian pronunciation which brought it out as 'Prouti's'. This Menelaus misinterpreted as 'Proteus', a name he knew as that of the sea deity to whom Poseidon had granted the gift of prophecy. So, the combination of an old man's diction and Menelaus' mishearing gave the world the name of Pharos for the island with its patron deity being Proteus. Added to which, upon his return to Greece, Menelaus embroidered the story a little more and the seals that had bored Helen became transformed into nymphs who infested the beaches.

In 332 BC Alexander III, the Great, of Macedon 'liberated' Egypt from her Persian overlords who themselves had succeeded the last of the native pharaohs, Nectanebo II of the Thirtieth Dynasty, in 343 BC. Alexander was in Egypt only a matter of months before he pressed on with his attack against the Persian Great King, Darius, but he made a lasting impact there and thus on western civilisation. When Alexander arrived in Egypt the island of Pharos was simply known as the home of the sea-god Proteus. It stood a little offshore before the western mouth of the Delta and there was only a small fishing village called Rhacotis on a narrow strip of land between the sea and a large inland lake, Mareotis. In the autumn of 332 BC Alexander marched from Memphis, the ancient capital of Egypt (now just to the south of Cairo), along the western arm of the Nile to Canopus, a port on the great river that had long been used, and on towards the Oasis of Siwa in the western desert, via Rhacotis. His unerring eye immediately saw the potential of the wretched little fishing village site and he commanded a new city, Alexandria, to be founded there. This was the first of many cities that were to bear his name, but it was to remain always the mightiest of them all. He passed on to his destination, the Oasis of Siwa, site of the great oracular shrine of Ammon where, it is said, he underwent some traumatic and personal experience within the sanctuary and the priest in charge saluted him as the son of the god. Plutarch tells the story that the priest endeavoured to address Alexander in Greek as 'O, paidion' – 'O, my son' – but it came out as 'O pai Dios' – 'O, son of Zeus'. This made a lasting impression on Alexander, who henceforward saw himself as the son of Zeus-Amon, and his fight against Persia almost as a crusade or holy war. The Egyptians accepted Alexander as pharaoh and the idea of his being the son of a god held no qualms for them as it continued the old Egyptian idea of royalty being god-conceived. On coins issued post-humously, Alexander was represented wearing rams' horns over his Macedonian royal diadem; they were symbolic of Zeus-Ammon, to whom the ram was especially sacred.

The new city that Alexander founded was designed by the architect Dinocrates of Rhodes, following the very latest principles of grid town planning that had been devised a century earlier by Hippodamus of Miletus, who had 'invented' the grid system of streets. The limestone ridge offshore that formed the island of Pharos, combined with the reefs at its western end, had made a harbour there since prehistoric times. This harbour Homer knew, apparently, and described it in the *Odyssey*:

> There is an island called Pharos in the rolling seas off the mouth of the Nile. . . . In this island is a sheltered cove where sailors come to draw their water from a well and can launch their boats on an even keel into the deep sea.

Strabo tells us that

> Pharos is an oblong island, is very close to the mainland, and forms with it a harbour with two mouths; for the shore of the mainland forms a bay, since it thrusts two promontories into the open sea, and between these is situated the island, which closes the bay, for it lies lengthwise parallel to the shore . . . the extremity of the isle is a rock, which is washed all round by the sea and has upon it a tower that is admirably constructed of white marble with many storeys and bears the same name as the island.

He goes on to describe how the coast is harbourless and low on either side with reefs and shallows so that those coming from the open sea needed a good clear marker to guide them safely in. The island was inhabited; there was quite a large native population on it and several tombs of Ptolemaic date (305–30 BC). Strabo goes on to note that in his day the island had been laid waste by Julius Caesar because the population had opposed him in his attack on the Alexandrians and had, naturally, sided with their countrymen and their queen, Cleopatra VII.

Once a mole had formed between the island of Pharos and the mainland two sheltered harbours were formed, the Western and the Eastern, one of which would always be available for shipping, depending on the prevailing wind direction (Figure 71). Behind these harbours the city grew up along either side of the broad Canopus Street that ran straight from east to west. The city was divided into five quarters, each named for the first five letters of the Greek alphabet. Strabo (*Geography*, XVIII, I, 7–10) gives a detailed description of the city, its advantages in having the sea before it and Lake Mareotis behind which linked with the canals from the Nile and made it a flourishing entrepôt, at first richer than its cousin on the coast:

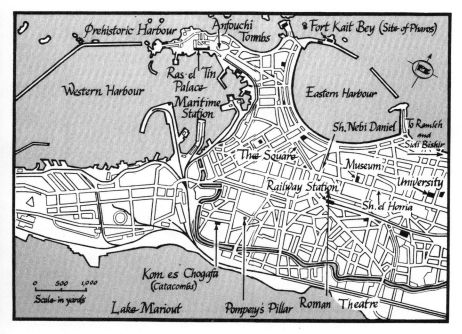

71 Plan of Alexandria. (Courtesy of Swan Hellenic Ltd)

The shape of the city is like a chlamys [military cloak]; the
long sides of it are those washed by the two waters [the sea
and the inland lake] having a diameter of about 30 stadia
[about 7000m]. . . . The city as a whole is intersected by
streets practicable for horse-riding and chariot-drawing . . .
the city contains most beautiful public precincts and also the
royal palaces, which constitute a quarter or even a third of the
whole circuit. . . . All, however, are connected with one
another and the harbour, even those that are outside the
harbour. The Museum is also a part of the royal palaces. . . .
The Sema also, as it is called, is a part of the royal palaces.
This was the enclosure which contained the burial-places of
the kings and that of Alexander; for Ptolemy, the son of
Lagos, forestalled Perdiccas by taking the body away from
him when he was bringing it down from Babylon . . . the
body of Alexander was carried off by Ptolemy and given
burial in Alexandria, where it still now lies – not, however,
in the same sarcophagus as before, for the present one is

141

made of glass [or possibly alabaster? Cf. the much earlier sarcophagus of Seti I, 1318–1304 BC, which is of thin, inscribed, translucent alabaster], whereas the one wherein Ptolemy laid it was of gold. . . . In the Great Harbour at the entrance on the right hand, are the island and the tower of Pharos.

Other major buildings at this later date of *c*. 20 BC included the Caesarium; the Emporium; the Heptastadium; Gymnasium; Hippodrome and the famous cult temple of the Graeco-Roman god Serapis, the Serapeum. Serapis is usually represented with a modius (a small corn measure) on his head as his particular attribute since he was the god of the corn supply, and Egypt had become the granary of Rome.

The Museum (a temple of the Muses) was essentially a monastic establishment where scholarship flourished and where accredited scholars were privileged with exemption from taxation and given free board and lodging. The other great institution in Alexandria was the Library – one of the two most famous in the ancient world (the other was at Pergamum in Asia Minor). It ultimately held some half a million scrolls (books were then written on rolls of papyrus or leather, papyrus being the obvious original material to use in Egypt, and a great source of income to the country). The Library was accidentally set on fire when Julius Caesar took Alexandria and it was burnt a second time by jubilant Christians in AD 391. These two institutions at Alexandria, the Museum and the Library, were a metaphorical beacon in the ancient world of learning; the literal beacon was to be supplied by the Pharos which was to give its name to the building and its use as a word for a lighthouse in many languages.

Descriptions of the Pharos occur in the writings of several of the classical authors around the beginning of the Christian era, notably Diodorus Siculus (*floruit* 60–30 BC); Strabo (*c*. 64 BC–AD 21), and the Elder Pliny. The latter, particularly noted for his great work the *Natural History*, was a man of acutely inquisitive intellect and this led to his death by asphyxiation in August AD 79 when he went to investigate the eruption of Vesuvius.

Who actually built the Pharos and the precise date of its erection are both a matter of some debate. It was apparently begun under Ptolemy I, Soter (305–282 BC), Alexander the Great's boyhood friend and famous general who, after Alexander's death in Babylon in 323 BC, acquired Egypt for himself. Ptolemy also 'acquired' the body of Alexander as it was making its way slowly back to the Macedonian royal burial ground at Vergina (where the tomb of his father, Philip II, has recently been found). Whilst the body lay at Memphis, the ancient capital of Egypt, Ptolemy carried out a historic 'body snatch' and took the corpse to Alexandria where it was to be interred in a grandiose mausoleum in the Sema. This has never been found although many searches have been made. In all probability it now lies beneath the sea since there has been considerable subsidence of the coastline at Alexandria since antiquity. To have the body as a focal point for a great mercantile and scholastic city was a great coup. The ever-increasing importance of Alexandria meant that its two harbours, another great advantage, had to be adequately 'sign-posted', since the Egyptian coastline is particularly flat and uninteresting in this area with few landmarks to guide the sailor to safe anchorage.

The building probably began in 297 BC, although the later chronicler Eusebius, Bishop of Caesarea (AD 263–339), who had been imprisoned in Egypt, mentions the building in his chronology for the year 283/2 BC. What does seem to be certain is that it was not built by Ptolemy, as has often been suggested. The name Sostratus is connected with the building, either as the architect or, as Peter Fraser suggests, the donor – a wealthy Alexandrian courtier who was also a diplomat. Strabo records (Book VIII, 25) that the dedication actually on the building read: 'Sostratus the Cnidian, friend of the sovereigns, dedicated this, for the safety of those who sail the seas.' Lucian (*c.* AD 115–180) gives it as: 'Sostratus, the son of Dexiphanes, the Cnidian, dedicated this to the Saviour Gods on behalf of those who sail the seas.' The 'Saviour Gods' could either be a reference to Ptolemy I, Soter (Saviour) and his wife Berenice who appear labelled as 'gods' (*theon*) on gold octodrachms (8-drachm pieces) issued by Ptolemy II. On the other hand, the Dioscuri, the Heavenly Twins, Castor and Pollux, who became the patron deities of navigation and had the specific function of rescuing sailors at sea, are often referred to in this form. However, the Dioscuri seem to be most unlikely in the context of Egypt. Posidippus, who had composed an epigram to celebrate the erection, or the completion, of the Pharos (and who is, therefore, the most reliable of the contemporary writers) invokes Proteus the sea-god whose home the island was and refers to the sailors' 'target' as Zeus Soter, Zeus the Saviour. For indeed it was Zeus Soter who acted as a marker on the very top of the

72 *Reconstruction drawing of the Pharos. (After Thiersch)*

Pharos on that long, low, undistinguished and flat coastline. The statue of Zeus Soter was on top of the Pharos from the first, and it was to him that the Pharos was dedicated (Figure 72). The tenth-century AD Arab historian, al–Mas'udi, refers to the inscription as being inset in large lead letters, each one a cubit (about 50cm, 20 inches) wide. It was located on the east side of the Pharos, where it could be easily seen by everyone entering or leaving the harbour.

Reverting to the question of who built the Pharos, Pliny the Elder specifically refers (Book XXXVI, 18) to 'the magnanimity that was shown by King Ptolemy on this occasion, he gave permission to the architect Sostratus, the Cnidian, to inscribe his name upon the edifice itself'. A Sostratus is known as an envoy of Ptolemy II, Philadelphus, at Delos in the 270s BC and it is a safe assumption that he and the man connected with the Pharos are one and the same. We have here a wealthy courtier/diplomat. Lucian (*Hippias* 2) mentions Sostratus of Cnidus as a famous engineer, linking him with Archimedes. He says that he helped Ptolemy capture Memphis by diverting the waters of the Nile. This cannot have occurred later than the death of Alexander, when Ptolemy was fully in control of Egypt, and so this famous engineer working for Ptolemy in the 330s can hardly be the same man connected with the Pharos itself. The ascription of the profession of architect to the later Sostratos by Pliny and others is a misunderstanding of the inscription and a mix-up perhaps with the earlier engineer. He could well be the engineer's grandson living in Egypt in the third century BC.

Posidippus' word, literally translated as 'set up', could equally be interpreted as either 'erected' or 'dedicated'. Added to which, it would be highly unlikely and unusual for the royal name to be omitted if Ptolemy I or II were the donors. It was certainly not the practice to record the architect's name on a monument in antiquity, although that of the donor/dedicator is obviously most necessary. The Pharos may have commenced building in the reign of Ptolemy I, Soter (305–282 BC) and was completed under Ptolemy II, Philadelphus (284–246 BC). It was apparently paid for and dedicated by one Sostratus of Cnidus, a wealthy courtier and diplomat (or possibly a merchant) and, in fact, we do not know the name of the architect concerned.

Now to turn to the actual structure itself. It is certainly amongst the earliest buildings in Alexandria of which we know; no doubt it was being built at the same time as the mausoleum, the Sema, was being prepared to receive the body of Alexander the Great. Since the Pharos was the first architecturally designed and developed lighthouse it obviously acted as a model, both direct and indirect, for others throughout the Graeco-Roman world, as can be seen from the evidence of surviving representations in mosaics and principally on sarcophagi reliefs. What we actually know about the Pharos, its specific physical appearance from written sources, as against debatable illustrations, is very little.

Pliny tells us that it cost 800 talents. A talent was a weight of silver, 581lb (25.4kg) avoirdupois, i.e. about 928ozs of silver (26,308 grams); this multiplied by 800 gives a cost of 742,400 ozs (21,046,668 grams) which works out at just over £4 million (at 1987 prices of silver bullion). Stories about the Pharos became embellished in the telling. According to Epiphanes, it was 306 fathoms high (1836ft or 559.6m!). Josephus, in his *Jewish War*, says that its light was visible from the sea at 300 stadia (about 54,864m or 34½ miles). Lucian of Samosata (AD 115–c. 180) extends that to 300 miles! Irrespective of the distance of visibility, they are all agreed that the light itself was provided by a huge fire in the base being reflected by mirrors from the top of the structure. Pliny notes 'that at the present day [mid-first century AD] there are similar fires lighted up on numerous places, Ostia and Ravenna, for example'. The lighthouse at Ostia is represented on the famous Ostia harbour relief in the Museo Torlonia, Rome, with tall flames emerging from the top. It also occurs on a bi-metallic medallion of the emperor Commodus (AD 177–192). Here we see the emperor welcoming the annual grain fleet into the harbour at Ostia, as he stands before a triple-tiered lighthouse (Figure 73). It is definitely the Egyptian grain fleet that he greets because the Graeco-Egyptian god Jupiter-Serapis, his corn modius (a measure of capacity) on his head, is distinctly seen steering the large galley on the left. Like many later lighthouses, the one at Ostia certainly copied in general form its famous predecessor at Alexandria which was, of course, still standing and in active use. Pliny goes on to say that 'The only danger is, that when the fires are thus kept burning without intermission, they may be mistaken for stars, the flames having very much that appearance at a distance.' This is still true enough of modern lighthouses seen on the far horizon at sea.

There is another interesting point here concerned solely with the logistics of the operation which does not seem to have been thought about previously – a vast amount of fuel, wood or charcoal, would be required to keep a continual fire alight and Egypt is not a country noted for its provision of timber. In fact, timber was very scarce in ancient Egypt (and still is in modern Egypt), the native trees then being only acacia and tamarisk, more scrub than tree. Dried animal dung could have been a possible

73 *Bi-metallic medallion of Commodus (AD 177–192) with the emperor standing before a three-tiered lighthouse in Ostia harbour to welcome the grain fleet from Egypt. (British Museum)*

solution to the problem and is still widely used in native houses today but, once again, the sheer quantity required presents problems. The presumption is that the intensity of the light was more a product of the reflection than of the fire itself. The reflecting agents would have been sheets of highly polished metal, probably burnished bronze, as were most mirrors in antiquity. In the daytime a far stronger reflection could be obtained by using the sun's rays. It is known that in the early medieval period heliograph messages of approaching ships were sent from the Pharos to the city of Alexandria. Since sailing by night was avoided in antiquity, the need for the light at night was second to the need for a beacon by day marking the way to the harbour of Alexandria.

To turn to the configuration of the building, it seems fairly widely agreed that it was a three-tiered structure with an overall height in the region of 100 metres: 60 metres for the first stage, 30 for the second and another 15 to the tip of Zeus Soter's trident or sceptre topping the third stage. Ancient and later Islamic sources are all agreed about the first and second stages but the Islamic version of the historian Ibn Tulun, and of the Fatimid restoration, placed a mosque on top of the third stage with a cupola tipped by the appropriate crescent symbol of the Faith. When this remodelling took place is not exactly known.

The entrance was not at ground level but raised a little at the head of a flight of steps. A number of similar representations of this style can be seen on several Roman sarcophagi reliefs. In the Ny-Carlsberg Museum, Copenhagen, there are three representations: one shows a draped female figure that may be intended to represent Isis Pharia (who will be discussed below) holding a three-tiered building on her outstretched right hand. Another relief shows a lighthouse at either end of a sarcophagus panel with three ships in between. The lighthouse seen on the left is an open-plan structure with a lattice-work parapet and a man standing there; the other is also triple-tiered and has flames issuing from its top. Numerous other such examples are known on later, principally Christian, sarcophagi.

On mosaics several lighthouses are depicted, many of them to be found on the floors of the small offices in the Square of the Corporations at Ostia, the port of Rome. Here, in the offices set around three sides of the square (there is a temple in the centre and a theatre at one end), were a number of mercantile concerns who featured several lighthouses of indistinguishable type on their floors. A sixth-century mosaic from Qars el-Libya, Cyrene, shows a crenellated structure labelled in Greek as a pharos and it apparently has two armed guards at the top. A mid-fifth-century mosaic found in Israel in 1964, excavated in the house of Kyrios Leontis at Beth Shean, has a curious juxtaposition of subjects. In the upper portion are Ulysses and the Sirens and down below a reclining figure of Nilus, the river-god, who holds a sacred ibis(?) out towards a small building with three storeys above a pitched roof and colonnade. Beyond it is a stylised representation of a Nilometer, marked off in cubits from 11 to 16 (the latter number being the optimum height of a good Nile flood, the annual inundation). Above the towered building is the word Alexandria set in the mosaic; presumably this is a very schematic representation of the Pharos. Another mosaic from Jerash in Jordan of c. AD 530 shows a crenellated town wall identified as Alexandria and the Pharos standing outside the wall. The basic elements of a triple-storey, and often a stepped approach, appear on a number of Greek Imperial coins which must all look towards the Alexandrian Pharos for their prototype. Examples are especially noted from Corinth (with her harbour at Lechaeum); Heraclea Pontica (Bithynia); Berytus and Laodiciea (Syria), Panormus (Sicily) and Aegae (Cilicia).

A fragment of a moulded and painted glass beaker found at Begram in Afghanistan (and now in the Kabul Museum) shows a view of the Pharos, clearly indicating its brickwork and rectangular windows all the way up the sides. A statue, presumably of Zeus Soter, stands on top and cradles his thunderbolt in his left arm. Other representations of the Pharos occur in three-dimensional form as terracotta lamps, and also as lampholders, from Egypt. However, the only piece of evidence that they add is that most seem to make sure of showing the numerous windows that rise up the sides of the Pharos to the lantern storey. Some earlier commentators have identified these as shields or bucklers hanging out on the surface of the tower, but this is not really acceptable.

The best and closest contemporary evidence for the appearance of the Pharos occurs on the Greek Imperial coins issued from the mint at Alexandria in Roman times. The Pharos appears as three main reverse types spanning the reigns of Domitian (AD 81–96) to Commodus (AD 177–192). Alexandria, operating as a mint

74 *Bronze half-drachms of Hadrian (AD 117–138) struck at Alexandria in years 11 and 17 showing the Pharos. The earlier piece (left) shows a profile view with a ramp ascending to the entrance. Both clearly show the Tritons at the top of the first stage and the statue of Zeus Soter on the top. (British Museum)*

within the Roman empire, as did many other cities of the Greek east, continued to strike coins of Greek appearance but bearing the reigning Roman emperor's head and his titles in Greek. The reverse designs (types) are interesting and, at times, a curious mixture of ancient Egyptian, Greek and Roman iconography. The Pharos appears first as a single structure alone; next in association with the goddess Isis Pharia and, last, with a galley sailing past it.

The series begins under Domitian where bronze pieces are known dated to years 12, 13 and 15 of his reign. (Alexandrian coins carry a regnal date in Greek letters, the regnal year running from 29 August to 28 August following.) The basic details of the structure are clear, especially the sea-monster Tritons blowing trumpets or long conch shells at the corners of the top of the first stage, and it has two stages/storeys only. The doorway is seen to be low at the base and a standing figure of Zeus Soter holding a long sceptre can be clearly seen on a number of specimens.

There is a gap in the reign of Nerva (AD 96–98) and the next coin representation occurs in the reign of Trajan (AD 98–117) when half-drachm pieces of years 11, 14 and 16 show a similar, perhaps not quite so stubby, building. Hadrian (AD 117–138) also issued the same types for years 2, 3, 6, 10, 11, 16 and 17 at least (Figure 74). Curiously, he does not seem to have issued the type for year 15, when he must have seen if not actually visited the

75 *Bronze half-drachms of Antoninus Pius (AD 138–161) struck at Alexandria in years 5 and 9. Both clearly show the numerous circular windows rising up the taller sides of the first stage and a high entrance doorway. (British Museum and author's collection)*

Pharos because in that year he made an Imperial visit to Egypt which is recorded on other coin types. In many instances these low bronze denominations have seen a great deal of circulation and consequent wear that makes it difficult to be sure of the particular date of the issue. One thing is certain, however: the basic form of the representation of the Pharos was always the same. We know from other architectural types that occur in the Greek Imperial series that an objective representation of the subject is invariably aimed at and there is a greater amount of accuracy in them than is often given credit.

On the coin representations of the Pharos up to and including the reign of Hadrian the entrance doorway is seen either at ground level or at least placed very low on the building. There is a change in the reign of Antoninus Pius (AD 138–161) when the doorway seems to have been moved rather higher up (Figure 75). This is, no doubt, an accurate rendition and may reflect some structural alterations carried out perhaps early in the reign. The type is known to have been issued for years 4, 5, 6, 8 and 9. A previously unpublished half-drachm of year 9 shows a particularly fine and clear representation of the Pharos with circular windows on the tall first stage and Tritons blowing their trumpets hanging off the upper edges, the doorway placed high up, and two very truncated

76 *Bronze drachm of Antoninus Pius (AD 138–161) struck at Alexandria in year 12 with Isis Pharia, holding an inflated sail and a sistrum, advancing towards the Pharos. The steps leading up the entrance are clearly shown. (British Museum)*

second and third stages, the latter topped by the statue of Zeus Soter. Marcus Aurelius (AD 161–180) also has a few half-drachms that include years 4 and 17, after which the Pharos disappears from the coinage as a single type.

A short distance away from Alexandria at Aboukir, the ancient Taporis Magna, is an interesting structure that is built over a tomb. It is quite close in shape to the Pharos and may be an example of a tower tomb being turned into a beacon. It appears to date from the late first century BC.

The second major coin type shows the Pharos with the standing figure of Isis Pharia (of the Pharos). The great mother goddess Isis of ancient Egyptian religion takes on several different aspects in the later classical world and here she is seen as the patron goddess of sailors holding an inflated ship's sail out towards the Pharos (except on a few rare drachm pieces of Trajan, where she is seen hurrying away from the Pharos with her head turned back towards it). She also holds a sistrum, a metal rattle, her sacred instrument that made a gentle tinkling sound when shaken. The reverse type of Isis Pharia always occurs on the larger flan bronze pieces, generally in parallel with the halves, although it is interesting to note that because of the height of the goddess the Pharos is seen similarly elongated. The same movement of the doorway to a higher point on the building may be noted on all the coins of Antoninus Pius (Figure 76).

It appears that Isis Pharia had a temple close by the Pharos on the island itself. Since classical times a lot of the Pharos island, indeed of ancient Alexandria itself, has disappeared beneath the

151

77 *Colossal stone statue of the goddess Isis recovered from the sea off Kait Bey fort and now lying in the garden of the Serapeum close to Pompey's Pillar at Alexandria*

waves as the coastline has subsided. Just off the edge of what was once the island (it has been joined to the mainland by a mole for centuries) evidence has been found by sub-aqua divers in recent years of a rock-cut temple. In 1963 some fragments of large letters in bronze were found, and in December 1963 frogmen lifted a colossal stone statue of Isis, nearly 10 metres tall, from the seabed. This must obviously be associated with her temple. The statue now lies just inside the entrance to the site of the Serapeum and Pompey's Pillar (Figure 77).

The third coin type with the Pharos shows it with a galley sailing past. It occurs only on a billion tetradrachm (four-drachm piece) of Commodus (AD 180–192) which is dated to year 29 (Figure 78). The apparent anomaly in dates is immediately explained by the fact that Commodus continued to use the regnal years of his predecessor Marcus Aurelius instead of taking his own from his accession on 17 March 180. He therefore starts his series of dates at year 21, and this type may be an allusion to a hoped-for

78 *Billion tetradrachm of Commodus (AD 180–192) struck at Alexandria in year 29 and showing a galley with an inflated sail passing the Pharos. (British Museum)*

imperial visit that did not come about in year 29.

The Pharos continued to be noticed in Arab historical sources and from them we know that it was badly damaged in an earthquake in AD 956 and yet again in 1303 and 1323. The fullest description of it that we have comes not from the classical authors already mentioned but from the Arab traveller Abou Haggag Youssef Ibn Mohammed el-Balawi el-Andaloussi who visited the Pharos as a tourist in AH 561 (AD 1166). He describes the island of Pharos as lying a little offshore and also mentions that it was possible to walk dry-shod over the mole or causeway at certain times when the sea was not too high. His description runs:

> The Pharos rises at the end of the island. The building is square, about 8.5m each side. The sea surrounds the Pharos except on the east and south sides. This platform measures, along its sides, from the tip up to the foot of the Pharos walls, 6.5m and rises above the level of the sea to an equal height. However, on the sea side, it is larger because of the construction and it is steeply inclined like the side of a mountain. As the height of the platform increases towards the walls of the Pharos its width narrows until it arrives at the measurements mentioned above.
>
> On this side it is strongly built, the stones being well shaped and laid and long with a rougher finish than elsewhere on the building. This part of the building that I have just described is recent because on this side the ancient work needed to be replaced.
>
> On the seaward wall, that is the south side, there is an ancient inscription which I cannot read; it is not a proper

inscription because the forms of the letters are carried out in hard black stone. The combination of the sea and the air has worn away the background stone and the letters stand out in relief because of their hardness. The A measures a little over 54cm. The top of the M stands out like a huge hole in a copper boiler. The other letters are generally of the same size.

The doorway to the Pharos is high up. A ramp about 183m long used to lead up to it. This ramp rests on a series of curved arches; my companion got beneath one of the arches and stretched out his arms but he was not able to reach the sides. There are 16 of these arches, each gradually getting higher until the doorway is reached, the last one being especially high. [This must be the staircase seen on the coins.]

They proceeded to explore the ruins on the island:

We penetrated about 73m beyond the doorway. Here we found a closed door on our left which led we knew not where. About 110m further on we found an open door. This we entered and found ourselves in a room, followed by another and others just the same for a total of 18 rooms along a corridor, all communicating with one another. Then we realised that the island of Pharos was uninhabited. Walking on for another 110m we counted another 14 rooms to right and left. In a further 44m we found 17 rooms. Eventually, after another 100m we reached the first stage [of the Pharos]. There was no stairway but a ramp that gradually ascended around the cylindrical core of this huge building. On our right was a wall that was not particularly thick and on our left the body of the building whose rooms we have explored down below. We entered a corridor 1.6m wide overhung with finished stones that formed a ceiling; two of my companions were not able to pass in it.

When we arrived at the top of the first stage we measured its height from the ground with a piece of string from which we hung a stone – it was 57.73m; the parapet being about 1.83m high.

In the middle of the platform of this first stage the building continued upwards, but now in the shape of an octagon with each face 18.30m long and 3.45m from the parapet. The wall was between 1.5 to 2m thick; the figure which I had written down in my original notes is not very clear, but close by where I had recorded the length of the string I had written details in ink, which had not smudged. This is most strange . . . but I am sure it was 2 metres.

This stage was taller than its base line. Entering we found a staircase which we counted as having 18 steps and arrived at the middle of the upper floor. We measured again with the string and found that it was 27.45m above the first stage.

In the centre of this platform on top of the second stage, the building continued upwards in cylindrical form with a diameter of 75.20m. From the foot of the wall to the parapet was 2.19m. We entered again and climbed 31 steps to arrive at the third stage. The height of the third stage was measured with the string as 7.32m. On the platform of the third stage there is a mosque built with four doors and a cupola. It is 5.49m high and 36.60m in diameter. The parapet is 46cm high and only 1.51m separates it from the mosque wall.

In summary, the structure that we had explored had 67 rooms, except for the first which we found closed and which, it was said, led underground to the sea. The height of the Pharos, following these dimensions, is 96.99m and, from its base to the edge of the sea, it is 9.15m; the portion that is visible below the sea level is about 1.83m.

This description and the measurements of the structure, linked with the pictures on coins and other media, gives us a very clear impression of its actual appearance. The lowest stage had a height of 57 metres and had a cylindrical core which bore the weight of the upper stages. The second stage was octagonal with a height of about 27.5 metres, with the third stage being cylindrical and around 7.5 metres in height. On top of this the coins show a gigantic statue of Zeus Soter that must have added at least another 5 metres to the height. Add to this the 10 metres that the base stood above sea level and we arrive at an overall height above sea level of about 117 metres.

The traveller Ibn Battuta describes the Pharos as being partly in ruins in 1326 and when he visited it again 23 years later in 1349 he found it 'in so ruinous a condition that it was not possible to enter it or to climb it up to the doorway'. A manuscript in the monastery of Montpellier gives the date of the destruction of the Pharos as 8 August 1303.

The latest reasonable representation that we have of the Pharos before its destruction is in a mosaic in the ceiling of the chapel of Zeno in St Mark's Cathedral, Venice, placed there about 1200 (Figure 79). It shows the Pharos and a ship with the Evangelist sitting in the stern as he arrives in Alexandria to found the Christian (Coptic) Church in Egypt. He died in Egypt and was

79 *The arrival of St Mark in Alexandria with his boat passing the Pharos, represented with the domed third stage, the mosque of Ibn Tulun's Islamic rebuilding. Thirteenth-century mosaic in the chapel of Zeno, St Mark's Cathedral, Venice*

buried in Alexandria. The mercantile Venetians, feeling that their need for relics of a saint were greater than those of Alexandria and Egypt, now under Islamic rule, stole the body of Mark in 868. It was taken to Venice where it now lies beneath the High Altar in the magnificent church that bears his name. The story goes that the wily Venetians smuggled the body past the Muslim customs officers by indicating that the casket holding the saint's remains was full of pork. Naturally, no self-respecting Muslim was going to doubt their word and investigate such an unclean cargo! Mark's removal was the second greatest body snatch in Alexandria's history, the first being Ptolemy I's acquisition of the body of Alexander the Great for burial there. Mark's skull was recently returned to Egypt from Venice and now lies buried in the Coptic Cathedral of St Mark in Cairo.

Today the site of the Pharos is covered by the great Islamic fort of Kait Bey, built in the fifteenth century on and from the ruins of the collapsed lighthouse (Figure 80). The area is a military one and difficult of access and there is little to see except the Islamic architecture. The memory of the Pharos is kept alive in Alexandria by a modern carving in white marble showing it and Isis Pharia as the tourist enters the gardens to visit the Kom-es-Shafur catacombs.

80 *Kait Bey fort, Alexandria, built in the fifteenth century on the site of the Pharos*

EPILOGUE:
SOME FORGOTTEN WONDERS

FROM THE second century BC onwards there was a great variety of lists of the Seven Wonders. The first actual mention of a select list showing an awareness that the idea of the Seven Wonders had entered popular consciousness occurs at the time of Julius Caesar in the first century BC. The historian Diodorus Siculus (of Sicily), in his description of a dramatic monument at Babylon, the great obelisk of Queen Semiramis, says that it should be numbered amongst the seven most notable works of his day. It is intriguing that he should make this comment about a monument that has now slipped from the list, but he was most certainly aware that it was fashionable to make a list of seven such monuments. Soon afterwards the geographer Strabo (64 BC–AD 21), a Greek from Amaseia on the southern coast of the Black Sea, stated that the pyramids were amongst a list of seven 'sights'. By this time the world of the Greeks had become subservient to the might of Rome. The empire founded by Alexander the Great had dissolved into a number of kingdoms, themselves often torn apart by political strife. One by one they succumbed to the influence of that new power from the west, Rome, which brought the whole of the Mediterranean basin into one political unit.

Again, a new vision of the oneness of the known world was apparent. Strabo's book was called *The Geography*, and it is literally a description of the world that he knew, from Spain to India, Europe and North Africa. It is a recital of human achievements in lands where relics of earlier cultures were fast disappearing. Such a work gives a fascinating insight into the world of the early Roman empire. His first-hand accounts of such monuments as the statue of Zeus at Olympia are invaluable in

81 *Relief, part of the monument of the Haterii, showing the Colosseum and nearby triumphal arches. Roman, first century AD. (Vatican Museum, Rome)*

allowing us to share the experience of being in the presence of one of the Seven Wonders of the World.

The idea of the Seven Wonders became increasingly more popular under the Roman empire. The poet Propertius, in the later first century BC, considered his verse to be more indestructible than the pyramids, the tomb of Maussollos, or the temple of Zeus at Olympia. The poet Martial in AD 80 actually saw the building of the Colosseum at Rome (Figure 81) and he could compare it with the pyramids, the city walls and the Hanging Gardens of Babylon, the temple of Artemis, the tomb of

Maussollos, and the horned altar on Delos – a list clearly selected to place the newly constructed Colosseum amongst the seven greatest buildings of all time.

The Seven Wonders thus became an integral part of Roman life and thought, although there was still no idea of a fixed canon. The list of monuments added to the smaller kernel of accepted wonders reflects the changing nature of the world. A work attributed to a certain Philo of Byzantium, an engineer of the late third century BC, is a generally flowery and inaccurate account entitled *The Seven Sights of the World*, and is written in a style quite unlike the real Philo's scientific approach. It probably is to be dated to the fourth century AD. Interestingly this reproduces the same list of Antipater of Sidon in the poem quoted here in the Introduction, but the descriptions were written more for their oratorical effect than as a true picture of the monuments themselves. It is, however, a firm list which must have been widely accepted at the time that it was written.

By the time of the Roman empire the Seven Wonders were themselves beginning to decay. Babylon was no more. The desert had reclaimed its great buildings. Even so, many who constructed lists of 'Wonders' looked back to the Persians, sometimes noting other monuments such as the palace of King Cyrus at Ecbatana. Some looked back to the Egyptians, and to their legendary city of 'hundred-gated' Thebes, as Homer had described it (Figure 82). Most, of course, turned to the achievements of the Roman world, to monuments such as the Capitol, the citadel of Rome with its great temple dedicated to the Roman triad of deities, Jupiter, Juno and Minerva (Figure 83).

In the fourth century AD Christianity made its mark on the Roman empire, and it is certainly through the interest of educated Christian writers such as Gregory of Nazianzus (AD 329–389) in past history that the idea of the Seven Wonders was kept alive. It is not surprising that with the changes that had taken place in the political world there was also a change in the attitudes of what should be included amongst the Seven Wonders. Another

82 *The Great Hypostyle Hall built by Ramesses II (1304–1236 BC) with the obelisk of Tuthmosis I (1525–1512 BC) in the temple of Amun at Karnak, Thebes. The site of ancient Thebes and its many temples, so highly praised in antiquity, was only rediscovered at the beginning of the eighteenth century by the Jesuit missionary Father Claude Sicard*

83 *Marble relief of Marcus Aurelius (AD 161–180) performing a sacrifice before the buildings of the Capitol in Rome. (Capitoline Museum, Rome)*

84 *Reverse of a bronze coin of Philip I (AD 244–249) with a representation of Noah's Ark. Struck at Apameia, Phrygia. (From an engraving published in 1775)*

Gregory, Bishop of Tours (AD 536–594), compiled a list of seven which included the Temple of Solomon at Jerusalem and Noah's Ark (Figure 84). The importance that such monuments may have held in the early Christian view of history can be appreciated, but their inclusion suggests a very different concept of the Seven Wonders from that of the earlier Greek and Roman authors. Gregory of Tours did not so much look around him to survey the marvellous sights and achievements of his world. Like the scholars of the later Renaissance and of today, he looked back into history to search for monuments of human achievement which may no longer have survived. Using the Old Testament as a source, he was able to choose the two monuments that stood out in Jewish tradition as vitally important in the history of humankind. At the same time, however, he was the first to name the Pharos as one of the Seven Wonders. He knew that it had given its name to all lighthouses, but he probably also knew that it was continuing to perform its original function although it had been built nearly a thousand years earlier.

With such a variety of monuments it is not surprising that a fixed canon of the Seven Wonders of the World was not agreed at that time. The idea continued to play upon the public imagination, even as the monuments themselves disappeared and the world that had once been united under Rome disintegrated into many different nations. Scholars looked back to the time when, it was thought, there was harmony in the oneness of the empire. Typical of the approach prevalent at that time is a work entitled *A Treatise on the Seven Wonders of the world fashioned by the hand of Men*, attributed to the church historian the Venerable Bede

163

85,86 *Maerten van Heemskerck's idea of the Pharos of Alexandria contrasted with Fischer von Erhlach's of a century and a half later (see also Figure 72)*

(AD 673–735), a Saxon monk from Jarrow near Durham. This fanciful list included the Pharos, the Colossus of Rhodes, and the temple of Diana (Artemis) at Ephesos. Besides these were also the Capitol at Rome, a statue of the Greek hero Bellerophon (who provided a prototype for the Christian St George), a stadium building at a city called Heraclea, and a bath house that is now no longer identifiable. Bede clearly had no contact with these monuments. He had selected them in a purely academic manner and their descriptions can only be called bizarre. Their very choice, however, illustrates how cultural contact was being lost with the great achievements of the Roman empire. Isolated in small communities and troubled by political instability, the peoples of Bede's generation were unable to recapture a true picture of the past, despite a longing to return to it.

It is difficult at any time to realize that buildings with which people are familiar will be destroyed and that the civilisation we

know will be changed beyond all recognition. Yet it is possible to reconstruct in an accurate manner some of the buildings of the past, even after their destruction. In the Renaissance the interest in the early Christian writers and in the world of the Roman empire was a spur to seek again a select list of monuments to celebrate the major achievements of mankind. It was not really difficult to make a choice from those that had been set aside by ancient authors who had known the monuments as they stood. The pyramids of Egypt had been recognized from the beginning. Babylon was represented by the Hanging Gardens, the conception and complexity of which staggered Renaissance minds even though they had no knowledge of the building itself. The statue of Zeus at Olympia, the temple of Artemis at Ephesos, the tomb of Maussollos, the Colossus of Rhodes and the Pharos provide a mixture of monuments and functions that represent many facets of the achievements of the ancient world. It is, perhaps, surprising that no monument was included to celebrate the engineering feats of the Roman world, but it must be that Renaissance scholars were aware that the idea of the Seven Wonders went back long before the heyday of Roman achievements, and they returned to first principles in their search (Figures 85 and 86). Van Heemskerck's romantic engravings were more closely related to

87,88 *The Renaissance view of antiquity seen in van Heemskerck's representation of Pheidias' statue of Zeus at Olympia is sharply contrasted with*

contemporary paintings than to a realistic view of the monuments themselves (Figure 89). Yet there was a growing interest in reconstructing a true picture of the past. Just before his death in 1520 Pope Leo X commissioned Raphael to reconstruct ancient Rome itself. This came to nothing, but the seeds of archaeological exploration are latent in the idea. Even von Erlach's reconstructions are tinged with that sense of balance and order that are the hallmark of the seventeenth century and it is only now, 300 years

the eighteenth-century projection by Fischer von Ehrlach which obviously incorporates details referred to by the ancient authors (cf. Figure 30)

later, that we are able to offer a reasonably accurate picture of how the Seven Wonders actually appeared (Figures 87 and 88). The future will certainly bring to light new evidence to allow us to paint in some details more accurately, but we have been able to offer here a general view of these buildings and statues and to give something of the feeling of excitement and awe that worked upon the peoples of ancient times when they found themselves in the presence of one of the Wonders of the World.

DIANÆ EPHESIÆ TEMPLVM

89 *The sixteenth-century idea of the temple of Artemis bears no resemblance to the evidence on the coins (see Figure 45), although Maerten van Heemskerck's engraving is very imaginative*

SELECT
BIBLIOGRAPHY

ANCIENT AUTHORS

Diodorus Siculus *Library of History*.
Herodotus *The Histories*.
Manetho *The History of Egypt*.
Pausanias *Guide to Greece*.
Philo *The Seven Sights of the World*.
Pliny the Elder *Natural History*.
Strabo *The Geography*.
Vitruvius *The Ten Books of Architecture*.
Note: Many of the above are available in modern translations in
the Penguin Classics series; others may be found in the Loeb
Classical Library (published by Heinemann).

CHAPTER 1   THE GREAT PYRAMID OF GIZA

Edwards, I.E.S., *The Pyramids of Egypt*, 1st edn, London, 1947,
    and many subsequent.
Jenkins, N., *The Boat Beneath the Pyramid: Cheops' Royal Ship*,
    London, 1980.
Mendelssohn, K., *The Riddle of the Pyramids*, London, 1974.
Petrie, W.M.F., *The Pyramids and Temples of Giza*, London, 1883.

CHAPTER 2   THE HANGING GARDENS OF BABYLON

'Alwan, Kamil, 'The Vaulted Structures or the So-called Hanging
    Gardens', *Sumer* 35 (1979), 134–6.

Koldewey, R., *The Excavations at Babylon*, London, 1914.

Nagel, W., 'Where were the "Hanging Gardens" situated in Babylon?', *Sumer* 35 (1979), 241–2.

Oates, J., *Babylon*, London, 1986.

Wiseman, D.J., 'Mesopotamian Gardens', *Anatolian Studies* 33 (1983), 137–44.

Wiseman, D.J., 'Palace and Temple Gardens in the Near East', *Bulletin of Middle Eastern Culture Center in Japan* 1 (1984), 37–43.

Wiseman, D.J., *Nebuchadnezzar and Babylon* (Schweich Lectures of the British Academy 1983), London, 1985.

CHAPTER 3   THE STATUE OF ZEUS AT OLYMPIA

Ashmole, B. and Yalouris, N., *Olympia*, London, 1967.

Kunze, E., *Neue Deutschen Ausgrabungen in Mittelmeerbegiet und in Vorderen Orient*, Berlin, 1959.

Liegle, J., *Der Zeus des Pheidias*, Berlin, 1952.

Mallwitz, A. and Schiering, W., *Die Werkstatt des Pheidias in Olympia*, Olympische Forschungen V. Berlin, 1964.

Richter, G.M.A., 'The Pheidian Zeus at Olympia', *Hesperia*, 1966, 166–70.

Swaddling, J., *The Ancient Olympic Games*, London, 1980.

CHAPTER 4   THE TEMPLE OF ARTEMIS AT EPHESOS

Bammer, A., *Die Architektur des jungeren Artemision von Ephesos* (Veroff. d. Deutsch. Arch. Inst.), Wiesbaden, 1972.

Cook, B.F., 'The Tympanum of the Fourth Century Temple of Artemis at Ephesus', *British Museum Quarterly* XXXVII (1973), 137–40.

Eckschmidt, W., *Die sieben Weltwunder, ehre Erbauung, Zerstorung und Wiederentdeckung*, Mainz am Rhein, 1984, 69–121.

Fleischer, R., *Artemis von Ephesos und verwandte Kultstatuen aus Anatolien und Syrien*, Leiden, 1973.

Foss, C., *Ephesus after Antiquity*, Cambridge, 1979.

Krischen, F., *Weltwunder der Baukunst in Babylonien und Ionien*, Tubingen, 1956.

Lessing, E. and Oberleitner, W., *Ephesos, Weldstadt der Antiche*, Vienna and Heidelberg, 1978.

Oberleitner, W. *et al.*, *Katalog der Antike Sammlung II, Kunsthistorisches Museum, Wien: Funde aus Ephesos und Samothrake*, Vienna, 1978.

Plommer, H., 'St John's Church, Ephesus', *Anatolian Studies* 12 (1962), 119–29.

Price, M. and Trell, B., *Coins and their Cities*, London, 1977, 127–32.

Trell, B.L., 'The Temple of Artemis at Ephesus', *ANS Numismatic Notes and Monographs* 107, New York, 1945.

CHAPTER 5   THE MAUSOLEUM AT HALICARNASSUS

Ashmole, B., *Architect and Sculptor in Ancient Greece*, London, 1972, 147–91.

Hornblower, S., *Mausolus*, Oxford, 1982.

Jeppesen, K., *Paradeigmata*, Aarhus, 1958, 1–67.

Jeppesen, K., Hojlund, F. and Aaris-Sorensen, K., *The Maussolleion at Halikarnassos. 1 The Sacrificial Deposit*, Aarhus, 1981.

Jeppesen, K. and Luttrell, A., *The Maussolleion at Halikarnassos. 2 The Written Sources and their Archaeological Background*, Aarhus, 1986.

Newton, C.J., *A History of Discoveries at Halicarnassus, Cnidus and Branchidae*, London, 1862.

Smith, A.H., *A Catalogue of Sculpture in the Department of Greek and Roman Antiquities in the British Museum*, London, 1900, 65–135.

Waywell, G.B., *The Free-Standing Sculptures of the Mausoleum at Halicarnassus*, London, 1978.

CHAPTER 6   THE COLOSSUS OF RHODES

Anthologia Palatina vi, no. 171 (for the Colossus dedication).

Clara Rhodos i (1928), 46; viii (1936) 245–87 (for the Italian excavations of the site of the Temple of Helios).

Clara Rhodos v, pt 2 (1932), 'Rilievo frammentario di Elios', 24–6, fig. 15 and pl. II (for the inspiration for Maryon's reconstruction).

Gabriel, A., 'La construction, l'attitude et l'emplacement du

Colosse de Rhodes', *Bulletin de correspondence hellènique* 56 (1932), 331–59.

Haynes, D.E.L., 'Philo of Byzantium and the Colossus of Rhodes', *Journal of Hellenic Studies* 77 (1957), 311–12.

Karousos, C., *Rhodes*, Athens, 1973.

Maryon, H., 'The Colossus of Rhodes', *Journal of Hellenic Studies* 76 (1956), 68–86, figs 1–3.

CHAPTER 7   THE PHAROS AT ALEXANDRIA

Bernard, A., *Alexandrie la Grande*, Paris, 1956.

Forster, E.M., *Pharos and Pharillon*, London, 1923.

Fraser, P.M., *Ptolemaic Alexandria*, Oxford, 1972 (repr. 1984).

Thiersch, H., *Pharos antike Islam und Occident: ein Beitrage zur Architekturgeschichte*, Leipzig and Berlin, 1909.

INDEX

Numbers in italics refer to illustrations